T0214511

SpringerBriefs in Computer Science

SpringerBriefs present concise summaries of cutting-edge research and practical applications across a wide spectrum of fields. Featuring compact volumes of 50 to 125 pages, the series covers a range of content from professional to academic.

Typical topics might include:

- A timely report of state-of-the art analytical techniques
- A bridge between new research results, as published in journal articles, and a contextual literature review
- A snapshot of a hot or emerging topic
- An in-depth case study or clinical example
- A presentation of core concepts that students must understand in order to make independent contributions

Briefs allow authors to present their ideas and readers to absorb them with minimal time investment. Briefs will be published as part of Springer's eBook collection, with millions of users worldwide. In addition, Briefs will be available for individual print and electronic purchase. Briefs are characterized by fast, global electronic dissemination, standard publishing contracts, easy-to-use manuscript preparation and formatting guidelines, and expedited production schedules. We aim for publication 8–12 weeks after acceptance. Both solicited and unsolicited manuscripts are considered for publication in this series.

More information about this series at http://www.springer.com/series/10028

Amit Vasudevan

Practical Security Properties on Commodity Computing Platforms

The uber eXtensible Micro-Hypervisor
Framework

 Springer

Amit Vasudevan
Software Engineering Institute
Carnegie Mellon University
Pittsburgh, PA, USA

ISSN 2191-5768 ISSN 2191-5776 (electronic)
SpringerBriefs in Computer Science
ISBN 978-3-030-25048-5 ISBN 978-3-030-25049-2 (eBook)
https://doi.org/10.1007/978-3-030-25049-2

This Springer imprint is published by the registered company Springer Nature Switzerland AG.
The registered company address is: Gewerbestrasse 11, 6330 Cham, Switzerland

To my loving wife, Deepa, who continues to transform my imperfections into perfections, just by the touch of her love.

To my dear sons, Arjun and Akshay, without whom this book would have been completed 2 years earlier!

And finally, to my brother and parents who are very surprised that I am an author (again!).

With my second book, the dedication to my family remains; they are always in my heart.

Foreword

My first direct interaction with Amit happened over a decade ago. It was early in my research career and, like many in a similar stage, I was a program committee member for a prestigious academic conference on systems. That meant I had to carefully review conference submissions to decide on merit, giving everyone a fair chance, and picking the papers that deserved to be published. One of the papers I had reviewed was Amit's.

He and his coauthors had crammed reams of detailed information into the measly 11-page submission limit. After they tightened the language and shrank the illustrations and still could not fit in everything they needed to tell a coherent compelling story, they started shrinking paragraphs here and there, shrinking possible white spaces, until they could barely pass the guidelines and test of the automated format checker at the conference submission website.

I was absolutely horrified! Feeling the burden of impartiality and equal opportunity weighing heavy on me, I was incensed by the apparent violation of the spirit of the guidelines. But I was conflicted, because I also loved the work. It was careful, principled, and used existing hardware facilities in an ingenious way to enable rich interaction between low-level and high-level software securely and efficiently. As the back-and-forths between the contact author, Amit, and the committee began, one thing was obvious: there was a lot of passion. Amit and his coauthors had something deep, complicated, and important to say; they felt it had to be said precisely and without compromise on detail and completeness; and they were willing to do all they could to say it well.

This book represents this opportunity. It distills and systematizes Amit's and his coauthors' research over more than a decade toward building system support below the operating system for secure and verifiable software. The micro-hypervisor, the star of this book, is at the core of this challenge. It provides necessary software functionality on which the entire software edifice above must rely to implement its services and to be kept accountable and honest. That is a key challenge: in a world of outsourced computing, it is not only applications but also the operating system that must be helped and contained, kept fast and kept in check. This fundamental tussle—performance versus security—is what drives the micro-hypervisor vision and informs its development.

It is not an easy vision to pursue. A micro-hypervisor runs as close as it gets to bare metal, without the niceties of an operating system below it. It must handle peripherals, obscure modes of hardware execution, the arcane workings of memory hierarchies, and the careful dance among the dozens of cores of a modern multi-core CPU. It must offer observable, possibly machine-checkable proofs of the security properties it claims, such as isolation and integrity. It must be bug-free itself. And that is the easy part.

At the same time, a micro-hypervisor must be invisible, have a small memory footprint, have negligible performance overhead, and be entirely functionality-transparent to the systems software above: an actual virtual machine monitor, an operating system, and the applications.

The uber eXtensible Micro-Hypervisor Framework (uberXMHF) is an admirable solution in this tussle. It combines efficient design with carefully structured interfaces and decoupled functionalities, with formal security guarantees, and blazing-fast performance. Although all systems research is the work of teams, not individuals, Amit was indeed the driving force of this work, responsible for the design and implementation of much of the output of the related research. After years of envisioning, prototyping, publishing, and evangelizing, Amit presents in this book the results of that influential work, and this time he has enough space to do it exactly as he enjoys: thoroughly!

The book starts with the fundamental ecosystem within which micro-hypervisors live, necessitating their position in the design space. It then presents the hardware environment in which a micro-hypervisor must operate and systematically builds the necessary and sufficient intuitive rules that a micro-hypervisor must follow to guarantee its security. The next chapter presents the micro-hypervisor itself, uberXMHF, with a careful design of its architecture and implementation. Finally, a number of applications for a diverse set of security-related functionality, built on top of uberXMHF, are presented in the final chapter of this book.

After that first stark introduction to Amit and to his enthusiasm for his research quest, all those years ago, I have been privileged to collaborate with him for much of the past decade. It is with great pleasure that I see this second book of his come to the world, sharing his vision for secure and performant systems software. I hope you enjoy it.

Google Brain, Mountain View, CA, USA   Petros Maniatis
July 2019

Preface

Competitive markets with low cost of entry, little or no regulation, and no liability will continue to foster innovative, attractively priced, large *commodity platforms*. Such commodity platforms are inherently *untrustworthy* in nature, comprising disparate hardware and diverse-origin software components with uncertain security guarantees.

This book discusses the uber eXtensible Micro-hypervisor Framework (UBERXMHF), a novel micro-hypervisor system security architecture and framework that can isolate security-sensitive applications from other untrustworthy applications on commodity platforms, enabling their safe coexistence and facilitating runtime monitoring of the untrustworthy components.

UBERXMHF focuses on three goals which are keys to achieving practical security on commodity platforms: (a) commodity compatibility (e.g., runs unmodified Linux and Windows) and unfettered access to platform hardware; (b) efficient implementation; and (c) low trusted computing base and complexity.

UBERXMHF strives to be a comprehensible, practical, and flexible platform for performing micro-hypervisor research and development. UBERXMHF encapsulates common hypervisor core functionality in a framework that allows developers and users to build custom micro-hypervisor-based (security-sensitive) applications (called "uberapps").

Book Contents and Structure

This book is a distillation of research and development efforts spanning more than a decade. We primarily focus on the high-level motivation, architecture, and application domains. The following is a roadmap to the subsequent chapters in this book.

- Chapter "Micro-Hypervisors: What? Why?": In this chapter, we discuss the what and why of micro-hypervisors. We present a discussion on competing system architectures and delineate the capabilities and importance of micro-hypervisors.
- Chapter "Integrity Protected Micro-Hypervisor on x86 and ARM Hardware Virtualized Platforms": We analyze the feasibility of constructing an integrity-protected micro-hypervisor on contemporary x86 and ARM hardware platforms, observing that without the fundamental property of micro-hypervisor integrity, no additional properties (e.g., secrecy, information flow, etc.) can be achieved. Based on our analysis, we describe a set of necessary rules that must be followed by a micro-hypervisor framework to maintain micro-hypervisor integrity.
- Chapter "The Uber eXtensible Micro-Hypervisor Framework (UBERXMHF)": This chapter presents the uber eXtensible Micro-Hypervisor Framework (UBERXMHF) that strives to be a comprehensible, practical, and flexible platform for performing micro-hypervisor research and development; it encapsulates common hypervisor core functionality in a framework that allows developers and users to build custom micro-hypervisor-based solutions (called "uberapps") while freeing them from a considerable amount of wheel-reinventing that is often associated with such efforts. We describe the implementation details on both commodity x86 (Intel and AMD) and ARM (Raspberry PI 3) platforms.
- Chapter "Micro-Hypervisor Applications": This chapter describes several micro-hypervisor-based applications ("uberapps") that employ uberXMHF and show-case the framework efficacy and versatility. These uberApps span a wide spectrum of security applications including application compartmentalization and sandboxing, attestation, approved code execution, key management, tracing, verifiable resource accounting, and trusted-path and on-demand I/O isolation.

Availability

We are encouraged by the end result—a clean, barebones, low trusted computing base micro-hypervisor framework for commodity platforms with desirable performance characteristics and an architecture amenable to manual audits and/or formal reasoning. Active, open-source development of UBERXMHF continues at: https://uberxmhf.org.

We welcome contributions from new developers, researchers, and pretty much anyone interested in low-level system security and tinkering. More information on how to contribute and get involved can be found at the aforementioned web portal.

Pittsburgh, PA, USA   Amit Vasudevan

Acknowledgments

Some might believe that this entire book is the sole responsibility of a single author. They would be wrong.

The author is especially grateful to his long-time collaborator and good friend Dr. Petros Maniatis, who incessantly urged the author to begin organizing his ideas and thoughts from when it all began!

The author is also grateful to the following collaborators whose insights and enthusiasm have greatly enriched the author's research work over the past decade: Drs. Adrian Perrig, Virgil Gligor, Anupam Datta, Sagar Chaki, Limin Jia, Leendert van Doorn, Bryan Parno, Jonathan M. McCune, James Newsome, Yanlin Li, Qu Ning, Zongwei Zhou, Miao Yu, Mr. Emmanuel Owusu, and Chen Chen.

The author would also like to thank Bill Hohl and Joe Bungo at ARM for generously providing technical information and research hardware and software in partial support of this work.

The last thank you the author would like to give is to his research colleagues at Software Engineering Institute, Carnegie Mellon University, Drs. Grace Lewis, Dionisio De Niz, Mark Klein, and Ruben Martins, for their unwavering belief and support towards the author's quest for building verifiable and trustworthy computing systems.

This research was supported by CyLab at Carnegie Mellon University (CMU), Northrop Grumman Corp., Intel Science and Technology Center (ISTC), and Google Inc. The views and conclusions contained here are those of the authors and should not be interpreted as necessarily representing the official policies or endorsements, either express or implied, of CyLab, CMU, Northrup Grumman Corp., Intel Corp., Google Inc., or the U.S. Government or any of its agencies.

Copyright

Contents

Acronyms

ACPI	Advanced Configuration and Power-Management Interface
AES	Advanced Encryption Standard
AML	ACPI Machine Language
API	Application Programming Interface
BIOS	Basic Input/Output System
CPU	Central Processing Unit
DMA	Direct Memory Access
DSDT	Differentiated System Descriptor Table
EEPROM	Electrically Erasable Programmable Read-Only Memory
IOMMU	I/O Memory Management Unit
IPI	Inter-processor Interrupts
KMS	Key Management System
MMIO	Memory-Mapped Input Output
MMU	Memory Management Unit
MSI	Message-Signaled Interrupts
NVRAM	Nonvolatile Random Access Memory
OEM	Original Equipment Manufacturer
OS	Operating System
PCI	Peripheral Component Interconnect
PKI	Public-Key Infrastructure
ROM	Read Only Memory
RTS	Root of Trust for Storage
SHA	Secure Hash Algorithm
SLoC	Source Lines of Code
SMI	System Management Interrupt
SMM	System Management Mode
SMRAM	System Management Random Access Memory
TCB	Trusted Computing Base
TPM	Trusted Platform Module
UEFI	Universal Extensible Firmware Interface
VM	Virtual Machine
VMM	Virtual Machine Manager

Micro-Hypervisors: What? Why?

Abstract In this chapter we will discuss what micro-hypervisors are and why they are important. We will present a discussion on competing system architectures and delineate the capabilities and importance of micro-hypervisors.

1 Introduction

Modern systems architectures can isolate security-sensitive applications from other untrustworthy applications of commodity platforms, enabling their safe co-existence (Chen et al., 2007, 2008b; Cheng et al., 2013; Hofmann et al., 2013; Li et al., 2014; McCune et al., 2010, 2008; McKeen et al., 2013; Sahita et al., 2009; Shinagawa et al., 2009; Steinberg and Kauer, 2010a; Strackx and Piessens, 2012; Vasudevan et al., 2013). This is necessary because large untrustworthy software components will certainly continue to exist in future commodity platforms. Competitive markets with low cost of entry, little regulation, and no liability will always foster innovative, attractively priced, large software systems comprising disparate hardware and diverse-origin software components with uncertain security guarantees. This is more so the case with current proliferation of open-source software systems and development communities.[1] In Butler Lampson's own words, "among software components, only the giants survive" (Lampson, 2004). Thus, our best foot forward is to protect trustworthy software components from potentially unsafe untrustworthy software components.

In order to protect trustworthy software components from adversary controlled large untrustworthy software components, we can leverage one or more of the following commodity system architectures as a foothold.

---

[1] https://github.com.

2   Operating System (OS) Kernel Architectures

An Operating System (OS) kernel is a computer program that is the core of a computer's operating system, with privileged (complete) control over everything in the system (Tanenbaum and Woodhull, 2006). On most systems, it is one of the first components loaded on system power-up (typically after the firmware/BIOS and/or a boot-loader). The kernel orchestrates the rest of the system start-up as well as input/output requests from the software. The OS kernel also forms a bridge between the software and the hardware and handles memory and peripherals like keyboards, monitors, printers, disk, etc.

The critical code of the kernel is usually loaded into a separate area of memory, which is protected from access by application programs or other, less critical parts of the OS. The kernel performs its tasks, such as running processes, managing hardware devices (e.g., disk and network), and handling interrupts, in this protected kernel space. In contrast, the user space is where end-user applications run (e.g., text editor, graphical user interface, etc.). This separation of privileges prevents user and kernel code and data from directly interfering with each other, potentially causing instability as well as preventing malfunctioning application programs from crashing the entire OS.

Intuitively, the OS kernel space can now be used as a foundation to develop system security mechanisms. Security-Enhanced Linux (SELinux) is one such Linux kernel security module that provides a mechanism for supporting access control security policies, including mandatory access controls (MAC) (NSA, 2019). Similar capabilities are provided by OS kernel extensions such as Solaris Trusted Extensions (Oracle Corp, 2019), AppArmor (openSUSE, 2018; Ubuntu Wiki, 2019), and Tomoyo Linux (NTT Data Corp, 2019). OS containers and virtual environments are further examples of how OS kernel features such as namespaces and resource groups can be used to enforce isolated execution capabilities (Doug Chamberlain, 2019).

While leveraging OS kernel features and privileges to facilitate security mechanisms seems intuitive, unfortunately the vast majority of commodity OS kernel implementation (Windows, Solaris, FreeBSD, Linux) run into millions of lines of code including supporting drivers and extensions. Having a plethora of privileged components running in a single address space such as the kernel means any issue with other extensions or the kernel itself can lead to blotching the security mechanisms offered by other extensions.

3   Micro-Kernel Architectures

Micro-kernel is the term typically used to describe an approach to operating system design by which the functionality of the system is moved out of the traditional *kernel*, into a set of *servers* that communicate through a minimal interface. There have been various micro-kernel-based architectures proposed in the literature (Accetta et al., 1986; Hansen, 1970; Hohmuth et al., 2004; Liedtke, 1993, 1996; Shapiro et al., 2000; Steinberg and Kauer, 2010b; Wulf et al., 1974), but they all have an overarching common goal of minimizing the amount of privileged code in kernel space, the trusted computing base (TCB), while pushing most of the functionality into (unprivileged) user space. Separation-kernels (Information Assurance Directorate, 2007; Rushby, 1981), Isolation-kernels (Whitaker et al., 2002), and Exo-kernels (Engler et al., 1995; Hennessey et al., 2016; Kaashoek et al., 1997) are low TCB OS kernel architectures that share a similar goal as micro-kernels.

A micro-kernel is designed for a specific platform or device and is only ever going to have what it needs to operate. The micro-kernel approach consists of defining a simple abstraction over the hardware, with a set of primitives or system calls to implement minimal OS services such as memory management, multitasking, and inter-process communication. Other services, including those normally provided by the kernel, such as networking, are implemented in user-space programs, referred to as servers.

Micro-kernels in principle allow security sensitive applications to be housed as deprivileged servers. Therefore, one compromised server cannot affect the others. Furthermore, the amount of privileged code is drastically reduced. However, micro-kernels typically demand software to be refactored to meet its interfacing requirements. Micro-kernels also treat everything as separate *hardware-enforced* containers, imposing significant costs (e.g., page-table management, context switching). Monolithic kernels, on the other hand, are designed to have all of their code in the same address space (kernel space), which some developers argue is necessary to increase the performance of the system (Russell, 2019). Some developers also maintain that monolithic systems are extremely efficient if well written (Russell, 2019). The monolithic model tends to be more efficient (Operating Systems/Kernel Models, 2019) through the use of shared kernel memory, rather than the slower IPC system of micro-kernel designs, which is typically based on message passing. Messaging bugs can also be harder to fix in the micro-kernel architectures due to the longer trip they have to take versus the one off copy in a monolithic kernel. Process management in general can also be complicated.

It is likely due to the aforementioned drawbacks that micro-kernel approaches have really not made it to upstream commodity operating systems today. A classic example in this context is the long-standing debate between Linus Trovalds and Andrew Tanenbaum on the design of the hugely successful Linux as a monolithic kernel rather than a micro-kernel (Torvalds and Tanenbaum, 2019).

4 Hybrid-Kernel Architectures

Hybrid-kernels are used in most commercial operating systems such as Microsoft Windows and its derivatives. Apple Inc.'s own macOS uses a hybrid-kernel called

XNU which is based upon code from the Mach kernel and FreeBSD's monolithic kernel (Apple WWDC Videos, 2017). They are similar to micro kernels, except they include some additional code in kernel-space to increase performance.

Hybrid-kernel architectures represent a compromise between pure monolithic and pure micro-kernel- based approaches. This implies running some services (such as the network stack or the filesystem) in kernel space to reduce the performance overhead of a traditional micro-kernel, but still running kernel code (such as device drivers) as servers in user space.

A few advantages to the modular (or) Hybrid-kernel are: (a) faster development time for drivers that can operate from within modules; (b) on demand capability versus spending time recompiling a whole kernel for things like new drivers or subsystems; and (c) faster integration of third party technology and development practices.

In hybrid-kernel architectures, modules generally communicate with the kernel using a module interface of some sort. The interface is generalized (although particular to a given operating system) so it is not always possible to create and use modules. For example, the device drivers may need more flexibility than the module interface affords. The module interface is essentially two system calls and often the safety checks that only have to be done once in the monolithic kernel now may be done twice.

Some of the disadvantages of the modular approach are: (a) with more interfaces to pass through, the possibility of increased bugs exists (which implies more security holes); and (b) maintaining modules can be confusing for some administrators and system developers when dealing with problems like symbol differences.

5 Hypervisor Architectures

A hypervisor or virtual machine manager (VMM) is a computer software which in conjunction with the hardware creates and runs virtual machines. A system on which a hypervisor runs one or more virtual machines is called a host machine, and each virtual machine is called a guest machine. The hypervisor presents the guest operating systems with a virtual operating platform and manages the execution of the guest operating systems. Multiple instances of a variety of operating systems may share the virtualized hardware resources: for example, Linux, Windows, and macOS instances can all run on a single physical x86 machine. This contrasts with operating-system-level virtualization, where all instances (usually called containers) must share a single kernel, though the guest operating systems can differ in user space, such as different Linux distributions with the same kernel.

Type-1, native or bare-metal hypervisors run directly on the host's hardware to control the hardware and to manage guest operating systems. For this reason, they are sometimes called bare-metal hypervisors. Notable examples of bare-metal hypervisors include IBM z/VM, Xen, Oracle VM Server, Microsoft Hyper-V, and VMware ESX/ESXi.

The other category of hypervisors are type-2 or hosted hypervisors. These hypervisors run on a conventional operating system (OS) just as other computer programs do. A guest operating system runs as a process on the host with the hypervisor abstracting guest operating systems from the host operating system. VMware Workstation, VMware Player, VirtualBox, Parallels Desktop for Mac, and QEMU are examples of type-2 hypervisors.

Hypervisor-based architectures for improving system security have been extensively explored in recent years (Xiong et al., 2011; Ta-Min et al., 2006; Dinaburg et al., 2008; Quist et al., 2011; Sharif et al., 2009; Chen et al., 2008a, 2013). These systems are designed to provide interesting security and functional properties including trusted user and application interfaces (Ta-Min et al., 2006), application integrity and privacy (Xiong et al., 2011; Chen et al., 2008a), debugging support (Fattori et al., 2010), malware analysis, detection and runtime monitoring (Dinaburg et al., 2008; Quist et al., 2011; Sharif et al., 2009), and trustworthy resource accounting (Chen et al., 2013). The aforementioned approaches leverage existing general-purpose virtualization solutions (e.g., Xen, VMware, Linux KVM) for convenience, but generally do not require such functionality.

Type-1 hypervisors such as Xen and VMware run into 100K source lines of code (SLoC). Type-2 hypervisors such as KVM include the entire OS kernel (in millions of SLoC) within their TCB. While recent efforts have tried to adapt the notion of modularity within hypervisors (e.g., Xen Xoar), they still do not disaggregate privileged (hypervisor) code; a vulnerability within which can bring the entire system down. Indeed, complexity arising from device multiplexing and increased TCB make general purpose hypervisor architectures prone to security vulnerabilities (Wojtczuk, 2008a; CVE, 2007a,b; Wojtczuk and Rutkowska, 2008; Wojtczuk, 2008b). Furthermore, the use of hypervisor technology by malware and rootkits installing themselves as a hypervisor below the operating system, known as *hyperjacking*, can make them more difficult to detect because the malware could intercept any operations of the operating system (such as someone entering a password) without the anti-malware software necessarily detecting it (since the malware runs below the entire operating system) (SubVirt, 2019).

6 Micro-Hypervisor Architecture

Micro-hypervisors combine the good attributes of micro-kernels and hypervisors in terms of a small privileged and trusted core while borrowing the notion of modularity. Micro-hypervisors are characterized by their support for a "rich" single-guest model where the micro-hypervisor framework supports only a single-guest and allows the guest direct access to all performance-critical system devices and device interrupts (Vasudevan et al., 2013; Vasudevan and Chaki, 2018). The single-guest model results in a dramatically reduced hypervisor complexity (since all devices are directly controlled by the guest) and consequently TCB, while at the same time promising near-native guest performance. The rich guest environment supported by a micro-hypervisor can be a traditional operating system (e.g., Windows, Linux), a (deprivileged) virtual machine manager (VMM) that in turn supports multiple guests (e.g., Nova (Steinberg and Kauer, 2010b)), or in principle a traditional privileged hypervisor that supports multiple guests (e.g., Xen, VMware).

The micro-hypervisor can then monitor the execution of the guest or portions of the guest via micro-hypervisor extensions. The micro-hypervisor extensions can either be operating at the same privilege level as the core micro-hypervisor or suitably deprivileged (e.g., SFI or hardware deprivileging) or even operating within the context of the rich guest environment itself.

The "rich" single-guest model has several advantages:

- **Dramatically Reduced Hypervisor Complexity and Consequently TCB:** Since most devices are directly controlled by the guest, a micro-hypervisor does not need to deal with per-device idiosyncrasies or perform hardware multiplexing—inherently complex mechanisms that can lead to security issues (Karger and Safford, 2008; Elhage, 2011). This results in a small and simple hypervisor code base which improves maintainability and makes it amenable to formal verification and/or manual audits to rule out the incidence of vulnerabilities.
- **Narrow Attacker Interface:** A micro-hypervisor interacts with the guest via a deterministic and well-defined platform interface thereby greatly reducing the attack surface for potential vulnerabilities.
- **Near-native Guest Performance:** All (device) interrupts are configured and handled by the guest without the intervention of a micro-hypervisor. This results in a near-native guest performance (the guest still has to incur the memory/DMA protection overheads which are minimal in practice (Vasudevan et al., 2013, 2016).

The past decade has seen a surge in terms of various micro-hypervisor applications on commodity platforms. We discuss several of them in the last chapter (Micro-Hypervisor Applications) of this book.

Table 1 Qualitative comparative analysis of monolithic, micro-kernel, hybrid-kernel, hypervisor, and micro-hypervisor architectures

	Monolithic kernels	Micro-kernels	Hybrid-kernels	Hypervisors	Micro-hypervisors
TCB	Large	Small	Medium/large	Medium/large	Small
	Large	Small/medium	Medium/large	Medium/large	Small
Runtime monitoring	Apps	Apps, comms	Apps, comms	OS, apps, comms, hyp	OS, apps, comms, hyp
Performance	High	Medium	Medium	Medium/high	Medium/high
H/W capabilities	High	Low	Medium	High	High

Apps = applications, comms = communications, OS = operating system, hyp = hypervisor

7 Qualitative Comparative Analysis

We now compare monolithic, micro-kernel, hybrid-kernel, hypervisor, and micro-hypervisor system architectures along the following axes:

- **Trusted Computing Base (TCB):** is composed of two attributes. (a) the raw source lines of code (SLoC) which indicate the size of the code-base, and (b) the architectural complexity which indicates how complicated the interactions among the components are.
- **Runtime Monitoring:** ability to monitor the executing applications, driver, and the OS kernel code and being able to insert non-invasive traps on existing code operating either in privileged or unprivileged mode for general behavior observation (e.g., what the code is doing) as well as accounting (e.g., what resources the code is accessing).
- **Performance:** the system runtime performance overheads.
- **Commodity Hardware Primitives:** The extent to which commodity hardware primitives can be utilized by the applications, driver, and OS kernel.

Monolithic OS kernels have a large size and large complexity due to their emphasis on generality (e.g., supporting a plethora of device drivers, file-systems, and legacy capabilities). Hybrid-kernels and hypervisors fall within the medium size and complexity bin, since they still need to support a subset of the device drivers as the monolithic OS. Micro-kernels and micro-hypervisors have both a small size and small complexity owing to the fact that all device drivers are out of their code-base and they rely on simple primitives for their operations (e.g., hypercalls, inter-process communication, and hardware traps). This makes micro-kernels and micro-hypervisors most amenable to formal reasoning and/or auditing to rule out possible vulnerabilities.

In the context of runtime monitoring, OS kernels can be used to monitor application execution in general. Micro-kernels and hybrid-kernels in addition offer the ability to monitor information flow (communication) between the applications. Hypervisors and micro-hypervisors offer the most capability in terms of being able to monitor portions of the OS kernel, drivers, applications, and in certain cases even a nested hypervisor.

When it comes to performance, monolithic system architectures triumph since all components are bound cohesively and often run in the same address-space and with the same privileges. Micro-kernels and hybrid-kernels take a performance hit due to their deprivileging and inter-process communication requirements. Hypervisors and micro-hypervisor achieve close to monolithic performance since they are able to leverage hardware capabilities (e.g., hardware virtualization) in order to run the operating system with only the required interception (e.g., hypercalls or intercepts iff a device is virtualized).

Finally, with respect to the usage of commodity hardware primitives, hypervisors and micro-hypervisors offer the most unfettered access since they leverage hardware support to run the guest unmodified and can expose a subset of the available hardware primitives to the guest. Monolithic kernel fall next in line in terms of being able to use most of the hardware functionality except for those reserved for hypervisor use (e.g., hypervisor mode execution). Micro-kernels only rely on message passing and hence their use of hardware primitives is limited whereas hybrid-kernels fall in between monolithic and micro-kernels in terms of the system hardware capabilities that can be harnessed.

References

Accetta MJ, Baron RV, Bolosky WJ, Golub DB, Rashid RF, Tevanian A, Young M (1986) Mach: a new kernel foundation for UNIX development. In: Proceedings USENIX summer conference. USENIX Association, pp 93–113

Apple WWDC videos (2017) "Apple WWDC 2000 Session 106—Mac OS X: Kernel" via YouTube

Chen H, Zhang F, Chen C, Yang Z, Chen R, Zang B, Mao W (2007) Tamper-resistant execution in an untrusted operating system using a virtual machine monitor. Technical report FDUPPITR-2007-0801. Parallel Processing Institute/Fudan University, Fudan

Chen X, Garfinkel T, Lewis EC, Subrahmanyam P, Waldspurger CA, Boneh D, Dwoskin J, Ports DRK (2008a) Overshadow: a virtualization-based approach to retrofitting protection in commodity operating systems. In: Proceedings of ASPLOS, Seattle, WA

Chen X, Garfinkel T, Lewis EC, Subrahmanyam P, Waldspurger CA, Boneh D, Dwoskin J, Ports DR (2008b) Overshadow: a virtualization-based approach to retrofitting protection in commodity operating systems. In: Proceedings architectural support for programming languages and operating systems

Chen C, Maniatis P, Perrig A, Vasudevan A, Sekar V (2013) Towards verifiable resource accounting for outsourced computation. In: Proceedings of ACM VEE. ACM, New York, pp 167–178

Cheng Y, Ding X, Deng R (2013) AppShield: protecting applications against untrusted operating system. Technical report SMU-SIS-13-101. Singapore Management University, Singapore

CVE (2007a) Elevated privileges. CVE-2007-4993

CVE (2007b) Multiple integer overflows allow execution of arbitrary code. CVE-2007-5497

Dinaburg A, Royal P, Sharif M, Lee W (2008) Ether: malware analysis via hardware virtualization extensions. In: Proceedings of ACM CCS 2008

Doug Chamberlain. Containers vs. virtual machines (VMs): what's the difference? https://blog.netapp.com/blogs/containers-vs-vms/

Elhage N (2011) Virtunoid: breaking out of KVM. DEFCON 19. https://www.defcon.org/html/defcon-19/dc-19-index.html

Engler DR, Kaashoek MF, O'Toole J (1995) Exokernel: an operating system architecture for application-level resource management. In: Proceedings symposium on operating system principles. ACM, New York, pp 251–266

Fattori A, Paleari R, Martignoni L, Monga M (2010) Dynamic and transparent analysis of commodity production systems. In: Proceedings of IEEE/ACM ASE 2010

Kaashoek MF, Engler DR, Ganger GR, Briceaso HM, Hunt R, Mazires D, Pinckney T, Grimm R, Jannotti J, Mackenzie K (1997) Application performance and flexibility on exokernel systems. In: Proceedings of the sixteenth ACM symposium on operating systems principles, pp 52–65

Hansen PB (1970) The nucleus of a multiprogramming system. Commun ACM 13(4):238–241. https://doi.org/10.1145/362258.362278

Hennessey J, Tikale S, Turk A, Kaynar EU, Hill C, Desnoyers P, Krieger O (2016) HIL: designing an exokernel for the data center. In: Proceedings symposium on cloud computing. ACM, New York, pp 155–168. https://doi.org/10.1145/2987550.2987588

Hofmann OS, Kim S, Dunn AM, Lee MZ, Witchel E (2013) InkTag: secure applications on an untrusted operating system. In: Proceedings international conference on architectural support for programming languages and operating systems

Hohmuth M, Peter M, Härtig H, Shapiro JS (2004) Reducing TCB size by using untrusted components: small kernels versus virtual-machine monitors. In: Proceedings SIGOPS European workshop. ACM, New York, Article 22. https://doi.org/10.1145/1133572.1133615

Information Assurance Directorate 2007 (2007) US government protection profile for separation kernels in environments requiring high robustness

Karger P, Safford D (2008) I/O for virtual machine monitors: security and performance issues. IEEE Secur Priv 6(5):16–23. https://doi.org/10.1109/MSP.2008.119

Lampson B (2004) Software components: only the giants survive. Comput Syst. Theory Technol Appl (9):137–145

Li Y, Perrig A, McCune J, Newsome J, Baker B, Drewry W (2014) MiniBox: a two-way sandbox for x86 native code. Technical report CMU-CyLab-14-001. Carnegie Mellon University, Pittsburgh

Liedtke J (1993) Improving IPC by Kernel design. SIGOPS Oper Syst Rev 27(5):175–188. https://doi.org/10.1145/173668.168633

Liedtke J (1996) Toward real microkernels. Commun ACM 39(9):70–77. https://doi.org/10.1145/234215.234473

McCune JM, Parno B, Perrig A, Reiter MK, Isozaki H (2008) Flicker: an execution infrastructure for TCB minimization. In: Proceedings European conference in computer systems

McCune JM, Li Y, Qu N, Zhou Z, Datta A, Gligor V, Perrig A (2010) Trust visor: efficient TCB reduction and attestation. In: Proceedings IEEE symposium on security and privacy

McKeen F, Alexandrovich I, Berenzon A, Rozas CV, Shafi H, Shanbhogue V, Savagaonkar UR (2013) Innovative instructions and software model for isolated execution. In: Proceedings international workshop on hardware and architectural support for security and privacy

NSA security-enhanced linux. https://www.nsa.gov/What-We-Do/Research/SELinux/

NTT Data Corp. TOMOYO linux. https://tomoyo.osdn.jp/index.html.en

openSUSE (2018) AppArmor. http://en.opensuse.org/AppArmor

Operating systems/kernel models—"Wikiversity". en.wikiversity.org

Oracle Corp. Understanding and using trusted extensions in Oracle Solaris 11. https://www.oracle.com/technetwork/articles/servers-storage-admin/sol-trusted-extensions-1957756.html

Recordings of the debate between Torvalds and Tanenbaum can be found at dina.dk Archived 2012-10-03 at the Wayback Machine, groups.google.com, oreilly.com and Andrew Tanenbaum's website

Rushby JM (1981) Design and verification of secure systems. SIGOPS Oper Syst Rev 15(5):12–21. https://doi.org/10.1145/1067627.806586

Russell M "What Is Darwin (and How It Powers Mac OS X)". O'Reilly Media. quote: "The tightly coupled nature of a monolithic kernel allows it to make very efficient use of the underlying hardware [...] Microkernels, on the other hand, run a lot more of the core processes in userland. [...] Unfortunately, these benefits come at the cost of the microkernel having to pass a lot of information in and out of the kernel space through a process known as a context switch. Context switches introduce considerable overhead and therefore result in a performance penalty

Quist D, Liebrock L, Neil J (2011) Improving antivirus accuracy with hypervisor assisted analysis. J Comput Virol 7(2):121–131

Sahita R, Warrier U, Dewan P. (2009) Protecting critical applications on mobile platforms. Intel Technol J 13(2):16–35

Shapiro JS, Smith JM, Farber DJ (2000) EROS: a fast capability system. SIGOPS Oper Syst Rev 34(2):21–22. https://doi.org/10.1145/346152.34619

Sharif MI, Lee W, Cui W, Lanzi A (2009) Secure in-VM monitoring using hardware virtualization. In: Proceedings of ACM CCS, pp 477–487

Shinagawa T, Eiraku H, Tanimoto K, Omote K, Hasegawa S, Horie T, Hirano M, Kourai K, Oyama Y, Kawai E, Kono K, Chiba S, Shinjo Y, Kato K (2009) BitVisor: a thin hypervisor for enforcing

I/O device security. In: Proceedings ACM SIGPLAN/SIGOPS international conference on virtual execution environments

Steinberg U, Kauer B (2010a) NOVA: a microhypervisor-based secure virtualization architecture. In: Proceedings European conference on computer systems

Steinberg U, Kauer B (2010b) NOVA: a microhypervisor-based secure virtualization architecture. In: Proceedings EuroSys conference. ACM, New York, pp 209–222

Strackx R, Piessens F (2012) Fides: selectively hardening software application components against kernel-level or process-level malware. In: Proceedings ACM conference on computer and communications security

SubVirt: implementing malware with virtual machines. University of Michigan, Michigan. Microsoft 2006-04-03. Retrieved 2008-09-15.

Ta-Min R, Litty L, Lie D (2006) Splitting interfaces: making trust between applications and operating systems configurable. In: Proceedings of SOSP

Tanenbaum AS, Woodhull AS (2006) Operating systems design and implementation, 3rd edn. Pearson, Upper Saddle River. ISBN-10: 0131429388

Ubuntu Wiki (2019) AppArmor. https://wiki.ubuntu.com/AppArmor

Vasudevan A, Chaki S (2018) Have your PI and eat it too: practical security on a low-cost ubiquitous computing platform. In: 2018 IEEE European symposium on security and privacy, EuroS&P 2018, London, United Kingdom, April 24–26, 2018, pp 183–198. https://doi.org/10.1109/EuroSP.2018.00021

Vasudevan A, Chaki S, Jia L, McCune JM, Newsome J, Datta A (2013) Design, implementation and verification of an extensible and modular hypervisor framework. In: 2013 IEEE symposium on security and privacy, SP 2013, Berkeley, CA, USA, May 19–22, 2013, pp 430–444. https://doi.org/10.1109/SP.2013.36

Vasudevan A, Chaki S, Maniatis P, Jia L, Datta A (2016) überSpark: enforcing verifiable object abstractions for automated compositional security analysis of a hypervisor. In: 25th USENIX security symposium, USENIX security 16, Austin, TX, USA, August 10–12, 2016, pp 87–104. https://www.usenix.org/conference/usenixsecurity16/technical-sessions/presentation/vasudevan

Whitaker A, Shaw M, Gribble SD (2002) Scale and performance in the Denali isolation kernel. In: Proceedings symposium on operating systems design and implementation. USENIX Association, pp 195–209. http://dl.acm.org/citation.cfm?id=1060289.1060308

Wojtczuk R (2008a) Detecting and preventing the Xen hypervisor subversions. Invisible Things Lab

Wojtczuk R (2008b) Subverting the Xen hypervisor. Invisible Things Lab

Wojtczuk R, Rutkowska J (2008) Xen 0wning trilogy. Invisible Things Lab

Wulf W, Cohen E, Corwin W, Jones A, Levin R, Pierson C, Pollack F (1974) HYDRA: the Kernel of a multiprocessor operating system. Commun ACM 17(6):337–345. https://doi.org/10.1145/355616.364017

Xiong X, Tian D, Liu P (2011) Practical protection of kernel integrity for commodity OS from untrusted extensions. In: Proceedings of NDSS 2011

Integrity-Protected Micro-Hypervisor on x86 and ARM Hardware Virtualized Platforms

Abstract We analyze the feasibility of constructing an integrity-protected micro-hypervisor on contemporary x86 and ARM hardware that includes virtualization support, observing that without the fundamental property of micro-hypervisor integrity, no additional properties (e.g., secrecy, information-flow, etc.) can be achieved. Based on our analysis, we describe a set of necessary rules that must be followed by micro-hypervisor developers and users to maintain micro-hypervisor integrity.

1 Introduction

Virtualization allows a single physical computer to share its resources among multiple *guests*, each of which perceives itself as having total control of its *virtual machine* (VM) (Popek and Goldberg, 1974). Virtualization is an effective means to improve hardware utilization, reduce power and cooling costs, and streamline backup, recovery, and data center management. It is even making inroads on the client-side. However, in all of these roles, the *hypervisor* (or *Virtual Machine Monitor (VMM)*) becomes yet another maximally privileged software component from the perspective of the guest's trusted computing base (TCB). This stands in direct violation of several well-known principles of protecting information in computer systems (Saltzer and Schroeder, 1975). In many scenarios, the hypervisor may support guests for two or more mutually distrusting entities, thereby putting to the test the hypervisor's ability to truly protect its own integrity and isolate guests (Anderson, 1972).

Unfortunately, today's popular hypervisors are not without their share of vulnerabilities (e.g., CVE 2008; Wojtczuk and Rutkowska 2008), and appear to be unsuitable for use with highly sensitive applications. Despite recent enhancements to hardware support for virtualization (Advanced, 2005; Intel, 2005; Robin and Irvine, 2000), low-level systems problems (e.g., System Management Mode exploits (Duflot et al., 2009; Wojtczuk and Rutkowska, 2009) and vulnerable BIOSes (Kauer, 2007; Sacco and Ortega, 2009)) continue to plague existing solutions. We distinguish between threats to *hypervisor integrity* and threats to

© The Author(s), under exclusive license to Springer Nature Switzerland AG 2019   11
A. Vasudevan, *Practical Security Properties on Commodity Computing Platforms*,
SpringerBriefs in Computer Science, https://doi.org/10.1007/978-3-030-25049-2_2

hypervisor and guest data secrecy, observing that an integrity-protected hypervisor is a necessary, but not sufficient, condition for maintaining data secrecy in the face of mutually distrusting guests. We define *integrity-protected* to mean that the hypervisor's code cannot be modified in any fashion and the hypervisor's data cannot be maliciously changed.

Are today's virtualization and security extensions to the x86 platform sufficient to maintain the integrity of a hypervisor? This is a challenging question to answer for current platforms due to their high complexity. Challenging practical issues that we need to consider include per-device idiosyncrasies that arise from devices that are not completely standards-compliant, and the need to offer the precise (i.e., bug-compatible) environment expected by unmodified guest operating systems.

Given the challenges in designing and implementing an integrity-protected hypervisor, we define threats to data secrecy and availability (such as covert channels, side channels, timing channels, and resource exhaustion attacks) to be outside the scope. Data secrecy and availability can be ensured only if the fundamental property of hypervisor integrity is realized. For example, without integrity protection, portions of the hypervisor that manage the isolation of memory pages between guests may be maliciously modified, thereby allowing one guest to make modifications to the code or data of another guest. These modifications may include releasing secrets.

We enumerate core system elements (e.g., buses and system components) required to protect the integrity of the hypervisor on both x86 and ARM hardware virtualized platforms (Sects. 2 and 3, respectively). We then present rules for an integrity-protected micro-hypervisor in Sect. 4. We believe our rules represent a strong first approximation of the necessary requirements for an integrity-protected hypervisor on today's x86 and ARM hardware. We write these rules as micro-hypervisor developers with years of experience investigating micro-hypervisor integrity. We leave for future work the demonstration that these rules are also sufficient.

2 Elements of x86 Hardware Virtualization

Our goal is to preserve the integrity of a hypervisor, i.e., preventing inadvertent or malicious manipulation of hypervisor memory regions (both code and data). Consequently, only system components that can directly access memory or mediate memory accesses become critical to preserving hypervisor integrity. AMD and Intel—the two major x86 CPU vendors that support hardware virtualization— design their CPUs to work with the Peripheral Component Interconnect Express (PCIe Budruk et al. (2004)) system architecture[1] and build on the existing

---

[1] Peripheral Component Interconnect Express (PCIe) is a successor to the Peripheral Component Interconnect (PCI (Shanley and Anderson, 1999)) system architecture.

non-hardware virtualized x86 architecture. Both the PCIe and x86 architectures define precise methods for moving data to and from system memory. This standardization serves as a guide for the remainder of this section. To maintain generality, where applicable, we adhere to the PCIe terminology instead of using CPU/vendor specific terms.

2.1 Overview

Current x86 hardware virtualization encompasses both hardware and software elements (Fig. 1). The hardware elements are connected via the PCIe bus (though both Intel and AMD employ proprietary buses—Quick Path Interconnect and HyperTransport, respectively—to connect the northbridge and southbridge).[2]

The Northbridge (or Memory Controller Hub—MCH—on recent Intel-VT platforms)[3] connects the CPU(s) (which include an integrated Memory Management Unit or MMU) and Memory/Cache. The northbridge also supports other performance-critical components such as the graphics controller.[4] The northbridge further contains an IO Memory Management Unit or IOMMU, which is responsible for managing Direct Memory Access (DMA) transactions between the Memory and all attached peripherals without intervention by the CPU.

The Southbridge (or IO Controller Hub—ICH)[5] supports less performance-critical IO capabilities such as some types of disk and network interfaces, USB, audio, and legacy ports such as the serial and parallel port. The southbridge also connects an optional Trusted Platform Module (TPM) which is used to measure a dynamic root of trust (which we treat in Sects. 2.2.2 and 4.1).

The software elements in the x86 hardware-virtualized architecture are the system boot and runtime firmware (BIOS), firmware code on various peripherals, power management scripts within the BIOS, memory regions belonging to individual VMs, and the hypervisor itself.

Throughout this paper we use the terms northbridge, southbridge, and IOMMU functionally rather than referring to physical components. As an example, on the recent AMD-V and Intel-VT architectures the northbridge and IOMMU are physically a part of the CPU. However, their functionality remains the same. The following sections discuss these hardware and software elements in the context of an integrity-protected hypervisor.

---

[2]While the PCIe bus is the industry standard for connecting various components in the system, both Intel and AMD platforms employ proprietary buses to connect the Northbridge and Southbridge (Quick Path Interconnect and HyperTransport).

[3]Recent Intel-VT platforms use the term Memory Controller Hub (MCH) in place of the Northbridge.

[4]Recent Intel-VT platforms use the term Graphics and Memory Controller Hub (GMCH) to describe a MCH with integrated graphics controller.

[5]Also called the IO Controller Hub or ICH.

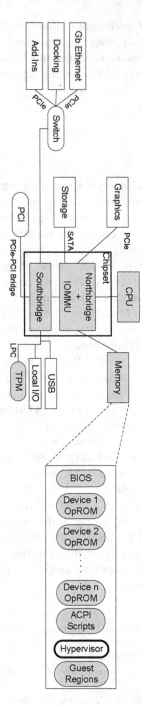

Fig. 1 Elements of today's x86 hardware virtualization architecture. Shaded regions represent elements that *must* be access-controlled to ensure hypervisor integrity. We discuss the TPM in Sect. 4.1

2.2 Hardware Elements

The hardware elements in the context of preserving hypervisor integrity are the CPU, Northbridge, and Southbridge.

CPU

An x86 hardware virtualization-capable CPU, like a normal x86 CPU, includes registers, caches, and an instruction set. The CPU has two over-arching operating modes: host (more privileged) and guest (less privileged). The guest mode is used to execute a guest OS environment in a controlled manner, i.e., in a virtual machine. The host mode can *intercept* certain critical operations that are performed in guest mode such as accessing CPU control registers and performing IO. There can be multiple concurrent guest instantiations, but only one host mode execution environment. Both host and guest modes can further execute in any of four privilege *rings* 0 (most privileged) through 3.

System Management Mode (SMM)

SMM code (part of the BIOS) executes at the highest privilege level and is used to handle system events such as system and CPU temperature control, and legacy support for USB input devices. SMM is entered whenever a System Management Interrupt (#SMI) occurs. The #SMI is an external hardware interrupt and can occur at any point during system operation. When SMM is entered, all normal execution state is suspended (including host and guest modes) and firmware code (#SMI handler) is executed with full access to system physical memory. The #SMI handlers are stored in a special memory region called the System Management RAM (SMRAM) which is only accessible by programming certain CPU registers or IO locations within the southbridge (Sect. 2.2.2).

Memory Management Unit (MMU)

The MMU is the CPU component that enables virtual memory management and handles all memory accesses from the CPU. Its main function is to translate virtual addresses to physical addresses using paging structures while enforcing memory protections, in both the host and guest modes. Recent x86 hardware-virtualized CPUs introduce the concept of hardware physical memory virtualization where memory addresses are separated into guest virtual, guest physical, and system physical. The guest virtual addresses are translated to guest physical addresses using guest paging structures. The guest physical addresses are translated into system physical addresses using another set of paging structures within the hypervisor.

Microcode

CPU microcode resides in a special high-speed memory within the CPU and translates instructions into sequences of detailed circuit-level operations. Essentially, microcode enables the CPU to reconfigure parts of its own hardware to implement functionality and/or fix bugs in the silicon that would historically require procuring a new unit. Microcode updates are loaded by the BIOS or the OS into the CPU dynamically.

All CPU(s) are shared between the hypervisor and the VM(s) that it runs, as the portion of the hypervisor that handles guest intercepts will always execute on the same CPU as the VM that generated the intercept.[6] This can lead to hypervisor integrity compromise if not managed properly. As an example, a malicious VM may attempt to manipulate CPU cache contents so that unintended code runs as if it is hypervisor code (e.g., Wojtczuk and Rutkowska 2009).[7] An attacker may also change existing SMI handlers in BIOS so that the malicious handlers execute as SMM code with sufficient privileges to modify hypervisor physical memory regions (Duflot et al., 2009; Wojtczuk and Rutkowska, 2009). An attacker can also alter a legitimate microcode[8] update to execute a CPU instruction that would normally be illegal and instead "trick" the memory caches into thinking the CPU is in host mode (SecuriTeam, 2004). From there, the attacker can gain access to hypervisor memory regions.

2.2.1 Northbridge

A *northbridge* (aka memory controller hub, MCH, or memory bridge) typically handles communication between the CPU, memory, graphics controller, and the southbridge (Sect. 2.2.2). The northbridge handles all transactions to and from memory. The northbridge also contains an IO Memory Management Unit (IOMMU) that is responsible for managing direct device accesses to memory via DMA.

IOMMU
An IO Memory Management Unit (IOMMU)[9] manages Direct Memory Accesses (DMA) from system devices. It allows each device in the system to be assigned to a specific *protection domain* which describes the memory regions that are accessible by the device. When a device attempts to access system memory, the IOMMU intercepts the access and determines whether the access is to be permitted as well as the actual location in system memory that is to be accessed. In systems with multiple physical CPUs, there may be multiple IOMMUs, but logical CPUs on a single die currently share an IOMMU.

---

[6]Even if the hypervisor is allocated a dedicated CPU/core, the portion of the hypervisor that handles guest intercepts will still execute on the same CPU/core of the VM that generated the intercept.

[7]This attack succeeds if the hypervisor page-tables for a guest map any of the hypervisor code pages with read permission. The code caches can then be manipulated as described by Wojtczuk and Rutkowska (2009) to run desired code as hypervisor code.

[8]Intel digitally signs microcode updates and hence altering a legitimate microcode update is not straightforward. However, AMD microcode updates are not signed, thereby allowing an attacker to freely modify bits (SecuriTeam, 2004).

[9]x86 CPUs also include a more limited graphics-related address translation facility on-chip, called a GART. However, unlike the IOMMU, the GART is limited to performing address translation only and does not implement protections.

Most devices today perform DMA to access memory without involving the CPU. DMA increases system performance since the CPU is free to perform computations, but a malicious device may attempt DMA to hypervisor memory regions, potentially compromising its integrity. As an example, FireWire is a serial bus that allows endpoints to issue remote DMA requests. One system may be able to issue DMA requests on the other system via the FireWire controller, thereby gaining read/write access to the full memory contents of the target and compromising its integrity (Boileau, 2006).

2.2.2 Southbridge

The *southbridge* (also known as the IO Bridge) is a chip that implements the lower-bandwidth IO in a system, e.g., USB, hard disks, serial ports, and TPM. It is also responsible for providing access to the non-volatile BIOS memory used to store system configuration data. The southbridge contains certain IO locations that may be used to compromise hypervisor integrity. For example, SMRAM access and SMI generation are controlled by IO locations that reside within the southbridge. An attacker could implant a malicious SMI handler by enabling SMRAM access (Duflot et al., 2009) and execute the handler by generating a SMI. The malicious SMI handler then has unrestricted access to hypervisor memory regions. Similarly, system configuration data copied from firmware into system memory at boot time can be manipulated using the southbridge, potentially preventing the BIOS from setting the system to a known correct state during boot-up.

2.3 Software Elements

In addition to the hardware elements that comprise the current x86 hardware virtualization architecture, there are various software elements. The software elements include firmware such as the BIOS, option ROMs, power management scripts that are embedded into the platform hardware, and OS and applications that run within a VM on top of the hypervisor. These software elements can contain bugs or can be altered to compromise the integrity of a hypervisor. Furthermore, certain software elements such as the BIOS and option ROMs execute even before a hypervisor is initialized and can set the system into a malicious initial state that compromises hypervisor integrity.

2.3.1 BIOS/UEFI

The Basic Input and Output System (BIOS) is by far the most prevalent firmware interface for x86 platforms. The BIOS prepares the machine to execute software beginning from a known state—a process commonly known as system bootstrapping. The Universal Extensible Firmware Interface (UEFI) is a specification that defines a software interface between an operating system and platform firmware (Intel Corporation, 2002). UEFI is a much larger, more complex, OS-like replacement for the older BIOS firmware interface but is only recently making its way into commodity platforms.

The BIOS is typically stored on a Flash (EEPROM) chip that can be programmatically updated. This allows for BIOS vendors to deliver BIOS upgrades that take advantage of newer versions of hardware or to correct bugs in previous revisions. Unfortunately, this also means that a legitimate BIOS can be overwritten with a malicious one that may compromise hypervisor integrity, e.g., hardware virtualization rootkits such as Blue Pill (Rutkowska, 2006) that emulate nested hypervisor functionality. Thus, an integrity-protected hypervisor thinks it is executing at the lowest level; Blue Pill code however has complete control over hypervisor memory regions.

Note that certain bootstrapping firmware such as Intel's EFI (Intel Corporation, 2002) and Phoenix's SecureCore BIOS (Technologies, 2009) only allow signed updates to the relevant Flash chip. However, since they have to include OEM customizable sections, parts of the BIOS image are not signature verified. Such areas (e.g., the BIOS boot logo) have been successfully changed by attackers to run malicious code (Heasman, 2007).

2.3.2 Option ROMs

A system can contain several BIOS firmware chips. While the primary BIOS typically contains code to access fundamental hardware components , other devices such as SCSI storage controllers, RAID devices, network interface cards, and video controllers often include their own BIOS, complementing or replacing the primary BIOS code for the given component. These additional BIOS firmware modules are collectively known as *Option ROMs*, though today they are rarely implemented as read-only, instead using Flash to support updates.

The BIOS invokes option ROM code for all system devices during bootstrapping. This gives the option ROMs the chance to intercept system interrupts and occupy system memory, in order to provide increased functionality to the system at runtime. The option ROM code is often legacy code that accesses physical memory directly. An attacker may replace a legitimate option ROM with a malicious one which may then be invoked at runtime by an OS running within a VM (Heasman, 2006a). This code can then have unrestricted access to hypervisor physical memory regions, thereby compromising its integrity. Certain BIOS code (e.g., Intel Active Management Technology) executes on a separate processor in parallel to the main CPU and can be used to compromise hypervisor integrity via DMA.

2.3.3 Power Management Scripts

Most systems today are equipped with power management capabilities where the entire system, including devices, can be transitioned into a low-power state to conserve energy when idle. Power management on current commodity systems is governed by the Advanced Configuration and Power Interface (ACPI) specification (Hewlett-Packard et al., 2006). With an ACPI-compatible OS, applications and device drivers interact with the OS kernel, which in turn interacts with the low-level ACPI subsystem within the BIOS.

An ACPI subsystem provides an OS with certain power management data structures in memory. A Differentiated System Descriptor Table (DSDT) provides power management code for system devices in a bytecode format called the ACPI Machine Language (AML). The OS kernel typically parses and executes the DSDT scripts to set device and CPU power states. Popular OSes such as Windows parse AML scripts in a CPU mode that allows accessing physical memory directly. An attacker that can insert malicious code within AML scripts will then have unrestricted access to physical memory when executed (Heasman, 2006b).

2.3.4 Other Code

A VM running on a hypervisor can run a full commodity OS. The OS itself may be subverted and may attempt to attack the hypervisor. As an example, malicious code within a VM may attempt to manipulate the caching policies of hypervisor memory, thereby effectively gaining access to hypervisor memory regions.

3 Elements of ARM Hardware Virtualization and Security

ARM's platform architecture comprises the Advanced Microcontroller Bus Architecture (AMBA) and different types of interconnects, controllers, and peripherals. ARM calls these the "CoreLink," which has four major components (Fig. 2).

- *Network interconnects* are the low-level physical on-chip interconnection primitives that bind various system components together. These include switches, bridges, and routing fabric. AMBA defines two basic types of interconnects: (1) the Advanced eXtensible Interface (AXI)—a high performance master and slave interconnect interface, and (2) the Advanced Peripheral Bus (APB)—a low-bandwidth interface to peripherals.
- *Memory controllers* correspond to the predominant memory types: (1) static memory controllers (SMC) interfaced with SRAM, and (2) dynamic memory controllers (DMC) interfaced with DRAM.
- *System controllers* include the: (1) Generic interrupt controller (GIC)—for managing device interrupts, (2) DMA controllers (DMAC)—for direct memory

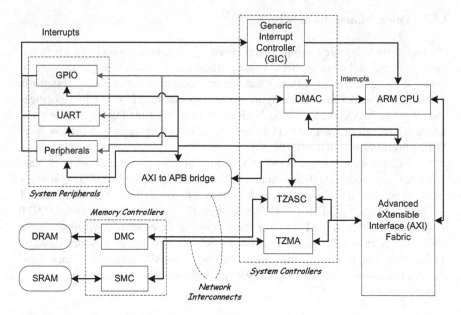

Fig. 2 Generic ARM platform hardware and security architecture

access by peripheral devices, and (3) TrustZone Address Space Controller
(TZASC) and TrustZone Memory Adapter (TZMA)—for partitioning memory
between multiple "worlds" in a split-world architecture (Sect. 3.1).
• *System peripherals* include LCDs, timers, UARTs, GPIO pins, etc. These
  peripherals can be further assigned to specific "worlds".

Multiple hardware primitives exist for isolated execution on ARM architecture devices today. ARM first introduced their TrustZone Security Extensions in
2003 (ARM Limited, 2003), enabling a "two-world" model, whereby both secure
and non-secure software can co-exist on the same processor. Today, TrustZone
features are available for many system components beyond just the CPU(s), as we
discuss below.

ARM also has hardware support for virtualization for their Cortex™ A series
CPU family based on the ARMv7 and ARMv8 architectures (ARM Limited,
2010c). These extensions enable more traditional virtualization solutions in the form
of hypervisors or virtual machine monitors (Popek and Goldberg, 1974).

3.1 Split-World-Based Isolated Execution

ARM's TrustZone Security Extensions (ARM Limited, 2009) enable a
single physical processor core to safely and efficiently execute code in two

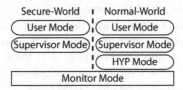

Fig. 3 ARM isolated execution hardware primitives. Split-world-based isolation enables both secure and normal processor worlds. Virtualization-based isolation adds a higher-privileged layer for a hypervisor in the normal world

"worlds"—the *secure world* for security sensitive application code and the *normal-world* for non-secure applications (Fig. 3). CPU state is banked between both worlds; the secure-world can access all normal-world state, but not vice versa. A new processor mode, called the *monitor mode*, supports context switching between the secure-world and the normal-world and can be entered either asynchronously (e.g., as a result of hardware interrupts or exceptions) or synchronously by the execution of the Secure Monitor Call (SMC) instruction. Note that the SMC instruction can only be executed from the supervisor mode (SVC) in the normal-world. The monitor mode software is responsible for context-switching CPU state that is not automatically banked.

3.1.1 Memory Isolation

ARM's TrustZone Security Extensions split CPU state into two distinct worlds, but they alone cannot partition memory between the two worlds. Memory isolation is achieved using a combination of TrustZone-aware Memory Management Units (MMU), TrustZone Address Space Controllers (TZASC), TrustZone Memory Adapters (TZMA), and Tightly Coupled Memory (TCM).

A TrustZone-aware MMU provides a distinct MMU interface for each processor world, enabling each world to have a local set of virtual-to-physical memory address translation tables. The translation tables have protection mechanisms which prevent the normal-world from accessing secure-world memory. Such MMUs employ tagged Translation Look-aside Buffers (TLB), where entries are tagged with the identity of the world. This enables secure- and normal-world entries to co-exist so as to improve performance (ARM Limited, 2009).

The TZASC interfaces devices such as Dynamic Memory Controllers (DMC) to partition DRAM into distinct memory regions. The TZASC has a secure-world-only programming interface that can be used to designate a given memory region as secure or normal. The TZASC rejects memory transactions from the normal-world that are directed towards secure memory regions. The TZMA provides similar functionality for off-chip ROM or SRAM. With a TZMA, ROM or SRAM can be partitioned between the two worlds.

Tightly Coupled Memory (TCM) is memory that is in the same physical package as the CPU, so that physical tampering with the external pins of an integrated circuit will be ineffective in trying to learn the information stored in TCM. TCMs are typically blocks of fast on-chip SRAM that exist at the same level as the CPU's L1 cache subsystem. Secure-world software is responsible for configuring access permissions (secure vs. normal) for a given TCM block.

3.1.2 Peripheral Isolation

Peripherals in the ARM platform architecture can be designated as *secure* or *normal*. Secure peripherals are intended to be accessible by the secure world while normal peripherals can be accessed from both worlds. Thus, there is a need to isolate secure and normal peripherals so that software running in the normal world cannot maliciously or inadvertently address secure-world peripherals.

ARM's "CoreLink" architecture connects high-speed system devices such as the CPU and memory controllers using the Advanced eXtensible Interface (AXI) bus (ARM Limited, 2010a). The rest of the system peripherals are typically connected using the Advanced Peripheral Bus (APB). The AXI-to-APB bridge device is responsible for interfacing the APB interconnects with the AXI fabric. The AXI bus transaction packets include an identification field that designates the transaction as secure or normal. However, the APB transactions do not have such a provision (ARM Limited, 2010b). This places the responsibility for managing security-relevant state with the AXI-to-APB bridge.

A TrustZone-aware AXI-to-APB bridge contains address decode logic that selects the desired peripheral based on the security state of the incoming AXI transaction; the bridge rejects normal-world transactions to peripherals designated to be used by the secure-world. A TrustZone AXI-to-APB bridge can include an optional software programming interface that allows dynamic switching of the security state of a given peripheral. This can be used for sharing a peripheral between both the secure and normal worlds.

3.1.3 DMA Protection

Certain peripherals (e.g., LCD controllers and storage controllers) can transfer data to and from memory using Direct Memory Access (DMA), which is not access-controlled by the AXI-to-APB bridge. A TrustZone-aware DMA controller (DMAC) supports concurrent secure and normal peripheral DMA accesses, each with independent interrupt events. Together with the TZASC, TZMA, GIC, and the AXI-to-APB bridge, the DMAC can prevent a peripheral assigned to the normal-world from performing a DMA transfer to or from secure-world memory regions.

3.1.4 Hardware Interrupt Isolation

As peripherals can be assigned to either the secure or normal world, there is a need to provide basic interrupt isolation so that interrupts from secure peripherals are always handled in secure world.

Hardware interrupts on the current ARM platforms can be categorized into: IRQ (normal interrupt request) and FIQ (fast interrupt request). The Generic Interrupt Controller (GIC) can configure interrupt lines as secure or normal and enables secure-world software (in monitor mode) to selectively trap such system hardware interrupts. This enables flexible interrupt partitioning models. For example, IRQs can be assigned for normal-world operations and FIQs for secure-world operations. The CPU core provides support for interrupt identification and redirection. For example, if an IRQ occurs during normal-world execution, it is handed over to the normal-world interrupt handler immediately. However, if an IRQ occurs during secure-world execution, the monitor-mode handler is invoked which can choose to handle the IRQ or inject it back to the normal-world. The GIC hardware also includes logic to prevent normal-world software from modifying secure interrupt line configurations. Thus, secure world code and data can be protected from potentially malicious normal-world interrupt handlers, but TrustZone by itself is not sufficient to implement device virtualization.

3.2 Virtualization-based Isolated Execution

ARM's Virtualization Extensions provide hardware virtualization support to normal-world software starting with the Cortex^{TM} A15 CPU family (ARM Limited, 2010c). The basic model for a virtualized system involves a hypervisor that runs in a new normal-world mode called HYP mode (Fig. 3). The hypervisor is responsible for multiplexing guest OSes, which run in the normal world's traditional OS and user modes. Note that software using the secure world is unchanged by this model, as the hypervisor has no access to secure world state. The hypervisor can optionally trap any calls from a guest OS to the secure world. We discuss the virtualization-based isolated execution in the context of the Cortex-A15 CPU and the ARMv7 architecture, but note that this applies to the recent Cortex A series CPU (e.g., Cortex-A53) and the ARMv8 architecture as well.

3.2.1 ARM Cortex^{TM}-A15

The ARM Cortex^{TM}-A15 processor architecture includes new capabilities for hardware support for virtualization. The A15 processor retains full compatibility with its predecessors (e.g., Cortex^{TM}-A9) and is based on the ARMv7 architecture. It includes hardware support for virtualization extensions which can run multiple OS binary instances simultaneously thereby enabling isolation of multiple execution environments and associated data. The Cortex^{TM}-A15 also includes support for multi-core processing and Large Physical Address Extensions (LPAE) which provides the ability to use up to 1 TB of physical memory. LPAE introduces 40-bit physical addressing that reduces address-map congestion by providing common global physical addressing while supporting multiple resident virtualized operating systems.

3.2.2   ARMv7 Virtualization Extensions

The ARMv7 Virtualization Extensions are similar to the x86 counterpart in terms of the high-level isolation and virtualization mechanisms. A new non-secure level of privilege level, called the *HYP* mode, holds the hypervisor. The ARMv7 hardware virtualization extensions provide various mechanisms for the guest such as interrupt masking, page-table management, and communication with system interrupt controllers (e.g., GIC) which avoid the need for hypervisor intervention during guest execution. It also provides configurable traps into HYP mode for various system control register accesses and instructions. The architecture also provides hypervisor support for guest instruction emulation via general constructs called *syndromes*. The ARMv7 virtualization extensions and the HYP mode are designed to co-exist with the TrustZone secure execution architecture as shown in Fig. 3.

Two-level Memory Virtualization

Before virtualization the OS owns the memory and allocates areas of memory to the different applications. Modern OSes commonly use virtual memory for address space separation. With two-level memory virtualization, the address translation is divided into two stages. Stage 1 translation is owned by each guest OS and Stage 2 translation is owned by the hypervisor. Tables from Guest OS translate Virtual Address (VA) to Intermediate Physical Address (IPA) and a second set of tables from the hypervisor translate the IPA to the final physical address (PA). The hardware allows aborts to be routed to the appropriate software layer (guest or hypervisor).

Interrupt Virtualization

An Interrupt might need to be routed to one of the current or different guest operating systems, the hypervisor or an OS running in the secure TrustZone environment. In the basic model of the ARM virtualization extensions, physical interrupts are taken initially in the hypervisor. If the interrupt should go to a particular guest, the hypervisor maps a "virtual" interrupt for that guest.

Virtualization Extensions provide the necessary infrastructure to aid in interrupt virtualization. More specifically there are special system registers and flag-bits that are banked (e.g., CPSR.I,A and F bits) which allow a particular guest to change these bits without the hypervisor needing to trap and emulate them. All virtual interrupts are routed to non-secure interrupt handlers in HYP mode (e.g., IRQ, FIQ, and Aborts). Finally, the guest manipulates a virtualized interrupt controller while the physical interrupt controller is in control of the hypervisor.

Device Virtualization Support and DMA Protection

ARM I/O handling uses memory mapped devices. Reads and Writes to the device registers have specific side-effects. Creating virtual devices requires emulation. Typically reads/writes to devices have to trap to the hypervisor which then interprets the operation and performs emulation. Perfect virtualization means all possible devices loads/stores emulated. Unfortunately, fetching and interpreting emulated load/store is performance intensive. ARMv7 hardware virtualized architecture introduces the "syndrome" construct to ameliorate this situation. Essentially, syndromes store information on aborts for some loads/stores. It unpacks key information about the instruction Source/Destination register, Size of data transfer, Size of the instruction, SignExtension, etc. which the hypervisor can readily use for emulation purposes.

Providing address translation for devices is an important aspect of any virtualization architecture since it allows containment of device memory accesses in order to enforce isolation. It also allows for unmodified device drivers in the guest OS. If the device can access memory, the guest will program it in the IPA.

ARMv7 hardware virtualization adds the option for a "system MMU" which enables second stage memory translations in the system for devices. A system MMU could also provide stage 1 translations allowing devices to be programmed into the guests VA space. ARM is currently defining a common programming model where the intent is for the system MMU to be present at the system bus level and configurable by the hypervisor.

4 Integrity-Protected Hypervisor

We now present our assumptions and the rules an integrity-protected hypervisor must observe, with related discussion. For the hypervisor to protect its integrity, it must ensure that it starts up in an unmodified fashion and continues to run without any inadvertent modifications to its code and data.

We assume that: *The target system on which an integrity-protected hypervisor runs is physically protected.* An attacker who can physically tamper with or replace with malicious versions system components. For example, on x86 platforms the attacker can physically tamper with the northbridge, southbridge, CPU, or TPM which in turn can successfully compromise hypervisor integrity. As another example, commands generated by the CPU during *root of trust* establishment (see Sect. 4.1) must reach the TPM with their integrity intact. The TPM connects via the Low Pin Count (LPC) bus to the southbridge. The LPC bus is a relatively inexpensive and low-speed bus in modern systems, and is thus susceptible to physical tampering. Therefore, the platform on which an integrity-protected hypervisor runs must be physically protected at all times.

The rules for an integrity-protected hypervisor can be divided into rules that must be followed for (a) startup, (b) runtime, and (c) hypervisor design (Fig. 4). From Sects. 2 and 3 we note that there are only two ways in which hypervisor memory

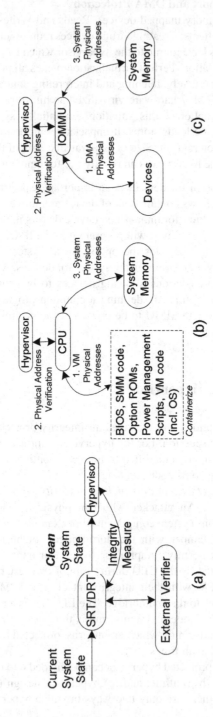

Fig. 4 An integrity-protected hypervisor: (**a**) must use a static or dynamic root of trust to startup, (**b**) must protect itself against any code via physical memory virtualization, and (**c**) must prevent any device in the system from directly accessing hypervisor memory. Finally, the hypervisor itself must be free of vulnerabilities

regions can be accessed on both x86 and ARM hardware-virtualized platform: (a) via code executing on the CPU,[10] and (b) via system devices performing DMA operations. Accordingly, we present the *exact* rules that must be followed by an integrity-protected hypervisor during startup and runtime, and consider its design in the context of cases (a) and (b) above. Consequently, a hypervisor that follows these rules is automatically protected from integrity compromise.

4.1 Startup Rules

These rules allow for the requirement that an integrity-protected hypervisor must start up in an unmodified fashion.

Definition 1 A *root of trust* (RT) is a trusted entity on the platform that acts as the starting point for trustworthy execution on the platform. There are two forms of root of trust entities as described below.

Definition 2 A *root of trust for storage* (RTS) is a trusted entity that provides confidentiality and integrity protection for stored information without leakage or interference of any form. Typically, elements called Platform Configuration Registers (PCR) and RSA asymmetric encryption is to protect data and ensures that data can only be accessed if platform is in known state (called "sealing").

Definition 3 A *root of trust for reporting* (RTR) is a component trusted to report to external parties information about the platform state accurately and correctly and in an unforgeable way using PCRs and RSA signatures.

Definition 4 A *static root of trust* (SRT) is an execution environment where the entire trust begins with the static, immutable piece of code, which is called Core Root of Trust for Measurement (CRTM). On x86 and ARM platforms the BIOS or the firmware is the first component to be executed. Therefore the Trusted Platform needs an additional entity, which would measure the BIOS itself and act as a CRTM. This entity is a fundamental Trusted Building Block (TBB) that remains unchanged during the lifetime of the platform. The CRTM consists of the CPU instructions that are normally stored within a chip on the motherboard. Alternatively, the CRTM can also be an integrated part of the BIOS itself.

Definition 5 A *dynamic root of trust* (DRT) is an execution environment created through a disruptive event that synchronizes and reinitializes all CPUs in the system to a known good state. It also disables all interrupt sources, DMA, and debugging access to the new environment. An explicit design goal of a DRT mechanism

---

[10]This includes code executing from the CPU caches. For example, an attacker could attempt to tamper with the execution of the hypervisor not by changing the memory of the hypervisor directly, but by changing the view of the hypervisor's code when it is executed on the CPU by tampering with the values stored in the CPU code caches.

is to prevent possibly malicious firmware from compromising the execution of a hypervisor.

Rule An integrity-protected hypervisor **must** be initialized via the creation of a static or dynamic root of trust.   □

Discussion: On many ARM platforms, the CRTM consists of an initial program loader which is embedded in read-only memory on the platform. This piece of code typically measures the first component before transferring control to it—called the *boot-loader*. The boot-loader can then establish a trusted measurement agent which can then store and (optionally) report on the transitive chain of component measurements as execution continues. The notion of static root of trust can also be applied to some embedded x86 platforms.

On commodity x86 platforms however, the traditional BIOS initialization and boot sequence is plagued by having existed for several decades. As such, modern security requirements and virtualization capabilities did not exist when it was first conceived. The result of this is that there may exist legacy code in a system's BIOS that should not be trusted, since it was never subjected to rigorous analysis for security issues.[11] Furthermore, many devices have option ROMs (Sect. 2.3.2) that are invoked by the system's BIOS at boot time. Thus, a malicious option ROM may take control of a platform before the hypervisor can be initialized. The dynamic root of trust mechanism provides a means for integrity-protected hypervisor initialization without breaking compatibility with myriad legacy devices.

Rule A root of trust mechanism **must** allow for an external verifier to ascertain the identity (e.g., cryptographic hash) of the memory region (code and data) in the new execution environment.   □

Discussion: In some cases the RT establishment can be unsuccessful (e.g., not all CPUs were able to synchronize). Furthermore, if the RT is successful, it only guarantees that the environment that is initialized is clean. The code that executes within the new environment may be a hypervisor whose integrity is already compromised. Therefore, there must be a mechanism to securely communicate to an external verifier whether a RT was successfully established, as well as a cryptographic hash of the code and data in the clean execution environment, so that the identity of the loaded hypervisor can be verified to be one known to enforce integrity protections. There are currently both hardware (TPM-based (Trusted Computing Group, 2007)) and software (Seshadri et al., 2005) based mechanisms for RT establishment either in a static (SRT) or dynamic (DRT) way. Both SRT and DRT mechanisms in principle include facilities to perform an *integrity measurement* of the new environment using the platform's hardware TPM chip or software TPM entity.

---

[11] For a closed system where only known firmware is executed at boot-time, a dynamic root of trust may not be necessary. However, most (if not all) x86 systems do not fall under this category.

4.2 Runtime Rules

Once an integrity-protected hypervisor has started in an unmodified form, it must continue to run without any inadvertent modifications to its memory regions (code and data). The following are the set of rules that must be followed at runtime by a hypervisor to ensure its integrity protection.

Rule An integrity-protected hypervisor **must** employ physical memory virtualization to prevent any code executing within a VM from accessing hypervisor memory regions.   □

Discussion: A VM running on top of an integrity-protected hypervisor can run any commodity OS and applications. Such an OS can use the BIOS, option ROM, and Power Management Script code during runtime. For example, Windows and Linux use PCI BIOS functions during startup and employ the video BIOS to control the video subsystem during runtime. Furthermore, it parses and executes Power Management Scripts as a part of system power management.

Code running within a VM may manipulate the MMU's virtual memory data structures to map and access hypervisor memory regions. Furthermore, it may disable virtual memory support and directly access system physical memory. Therefore, an integrity-protected hypervisor must verify any physical address originating from a VM before it reaches the memory controller. Consequently, an integrity-protected hypervisor must virtualize physical memory.

Definition 6 We define a *hypervisor core* to be the part of a hypervisor that is responsible for initializing, creating, and terminating VMs and for handling any intercepts that occur during VM execution.

Definition 7 We define *critical system operations* as operations that can result in compromising hypervisor integrity, e.g., changing page-tables mapping within a VM to map and access memory regions belonging to the hypervisor.

Rule An integrity-protected hypervisor **must** execute its core in the highest privilege level so it can interpose on critical system operations.   □

Discussion: An integrity-protected hypervisor is responsible for setting up guest environments, running them, and tearing them down. These operations require execution of privileged instructions and hence the hypervisor must be in an operating mode that allows the use of such instructions. Furthermore, an integrity-protected hypervisor must be able to detect any attempts to modify its memory regions by any other code within the system (e.g., code within the guest environments or device firmware). Thus, an integrity-protected hypervisor must execute in a CPU mode that enables the hypervisor to intercept and handle critical system operations such as device IO and writing to CPU control registers. Other parts of the hypervisor can execute at lower privilege levels contingent on hypervisor design.

Definition 8 Critical CPU registers are the set of CPU registers that can be used to compromise the integrity of a hypervisor. For example, on the x86 hardware virtualized architecture they can be divided into: (1) control registers—used for controlling the general behavior of the CPU such as interrupt control, switching the addressing mode (16/32/64-bit), and floating-point/multimedia unit control, (2) segment registers—used to define the memory region and access type for code, data and stack segments, (3) debug registers—used for debugging purposes, and (4) machine specific registers (MSR)—special-purpose control registers exposing CPU implementation-specific features. For example, MSR_EFER is used on both Intel-VT and AMD-V CPUs to enable extended features such as NX (no-execute) memory protections. While ARM hardware virtualized architecture have banked registers in hardware, they still share common control and debug registers.

Rule An integrity-protected hypervisor **must** have an independent set of critical CPU registers and **must** sanitize values of CPU data registers during control transfers to and from VMs.   □

Discussion: Sharing critical CPU registers between the hypervisor and a VM can lead to hypervisor integrity compromise. Code within a VM may use the control registers to turn off MMU-based virtual memory and set the data segment to address all of physical memory to gain access to hypervisor physical memory regions. Certain MSRs are employed by the CPU to save host mode state. As an example, on x86 AMD-V CPUs, the VM_HSAVE MSR is used to set the host mode save area which describes the physical memory region used to save certain host mode runtime state. A guest environment that can change the contents of this MSR can then change the host mode registers and compromise hypervisor integrity. Memory Type Range Registers (MTRRs) are another type of MSR on x86 platforms which are used to set caching policy for a range of physical memory. A guest environment can setup the MTRRs such that the CPU cache contents can be accessed and manipulated at runtime (Wojtczuk and Rutkowska, 2009). Since parts of hypervisor code and data will often be in the CPU cache, such MTRR manipulation can be used to compromise hypervisor integrity if the hypervisor's page-tables for a guest map hypervisor code or data with read permissions.[12] Therefore, an integrity-protected hypervisor must have an independent set of critical CPU registers which are *always* in effect when the CPU is operating in the host mode.

The CPU data registers are used for data movements to and from system memory. Data registers can be divided into: integer, floating-point, and multimedia registers. Guest modes can run a full-fledged OS which typically use these data registers for their functioning. If a hypervisor uses these registers (or a subset of them) for its operation, values of these registers carried over from the guest environment during an intercept can result in the compromise of hypervisor data integrity. Therefore, an integrity-protected hypervisor must either set data registers to a defined state (e.g.,

---

[12]Note that an adversary cannot exploit cache synchronization protocols in multi-core CPUs in order to manipulate CPU cache contents. All current x86 CPUs supporting hardware virtualization implement cache coherency in hardware, thereby maintaining a uniform view of main memory.

zero them) or save and restore contents of used data registers during control transfers to and from guest modes.

Rule An integrity-protected hypervisor **requires** the MMU to maintain independent states for the hypervisor and guest environments.   □

Discussion: The MMU is the CPU component that includes support for virtual memory (using paging) and memory access protections. The MMU interface is exposed via a set of CPU registers. The MMU also employs a Translation Lookaside Buffer (TLB) for caching address translations when using virtual memory. Since the MMU is involved in nearly every instruction that is executed by the CPU, a guest environment can compromise hypervisor memory regions if the MMU register set and internal states are shared between host and guest modes. As an example, if a hypervisor does not have its own TLB, the TLB entry loaded in guest mode can lead to unexpected address translations or access permissions. Therefore, an integrity-protected hypervisor needs the MMU on the CPU to maintain independent states for the hypervisor and guest environments.

Rule An integrity-protected hypervisor **must** intercept all hardware virtualization instructions.   □

Discussion: Both x86 and ARM hardware virtualized platforms provide a set of virtualization specific instructions that are used to create, modify, run, and terminate guest environments and to save and load guest environment states. A hypervisor can be compromised if these instructions are allowed to execute within a guest environment. For example, a guest environment could load its own state devoid of protections set by the hypervisor. However, an integrity-protected hypervisor can choose to implement recursive virtualization by emulating such instructions.

Definition 9 We define *containerization* as the process by which a hypervisor isolates some given code and associated data and executes them under complete control.

Rule An integrity-protected hypervisor **must** containerize any firmware, System Management Mode code and BIOS, option ROM or Power Management Scripts it uses.   □

Discussion: Firmware, SMM code, BIOS, option ROMs, and Power Management Scripts are low-level code that have unrestricted access to all system resources such as critical CPU registers, memory, and device IO locations. For example, a buggy or malicious #SMI handler can therefore access memory regions belonging to the hypervisor and compromise its integrity (Duflot et al., 2009; Wojtczuk and Rutkowska, 2009). Malicious code can also be embedded within the BIOS, option ROM, or Power Management Scripts (Heasman, 2006a,b, 2007) and these in turn can alter hypervisor memory regions. Therefore, if an integrity-protected hypervisor requires the use of BIOS, option ROM, or Power Management Script code, it must run them in isolation (e.g., in a VM). Furthermore, since #SMIs can occur at any point during system operation, an integrity-protected hypervisor must always containerize any SMM code regardless of the CPU operating mode.

Rule An integrity-protected hypervisor **must** prevent system devices from directly accessing hypervisor memory.   □

Discussion: An integrity-protected hypervisor can choose to let a VM use a physical device without employing any form of device virtualization. Alternatively, the hypervisor might need to virtualize a physical device and let the VM use a virtual device. As an example, in many systems, a single physical USB controller device controls all the available USB ports. The only way to share the USB ports between VMs would be to present each VM with its own virtual USB controller device that then controls a subset of the physical USB ports on the system. The virtual USB controller devices reside within the hypervisor and interpose on the USB protocol and direct the requests to the appropriate physical USB controller.

USB, FireWire, Storage, and Network devices can directly access physical memory via DMA, potentially bypassing the hypervisor. These devices can be programmed by an attacker to access any portion of the physical memory including those belonging to the hypervisor (Boileau, 2006). Malicious firmware on a device can also accomplish the same goal by replacing legitimate physical memory addresses passed to it with hypervisor physical memory regions. Therefore, an integrity-protected hypervisor must prevent devices from directly accessing its memory regions.

Rule An integrity-protected hypervisor **must** enumerate all system devices at startup and be able to detect hot-plug devices at runtime.   □

Discussion: As discussed in the previous rule, an integrity-protected hypervisor must restrict devices from accessing hypervisor memory regions. This requires the hypervisor to configure memory access restrictions for every device within the system. Consequently, the hypervisor needs to uniquely identify each device. While a device can be uniquely identified (e.g., the bus, device and function triad on a PCIe bus), the identification can change depending on system configuration. As an example, the triad on the PCIe bus is dependent on the physical location of the device on the system board, which may change between hardware upgrades. Therefore, an integrity-protected hypervisor must always enumerate all system devices during its startup to configure permissible memory regions for each device. Furthermore, with hot-plugging capabilities in current systems (where a device can be added or removed from the system at runtime), an integrity-protected hypervisor must be able to dynamically detect such additions and removals and enforce memory access restrictions for such devices. (An alternative, non-technical solution is to maintain stringent physical security to prevent devices from being hot-plugged. This may not be economical in practice.)

Definition 10 We define critical system devices to be devices that must be properly managed to prevent hypervisor integrity compromise. As an example, on the x86 hardware-virtualized architecture, these devices are the functional equivalents of the northbridge, southbridge, and IOMMU, as they can constrain the behavior of all other devices.

Rule An integrity-protected hypervisor **must** prevent access to critical system devices at all times.   □

Discussion: Critical system devices, like any other device, can expose their interface through either legacy IO or memory-mapped IO. For example, x86 Intel-VT systems expose the IOMMU as a DMA device through ACPI while x86 AMD-V systems expose the IOMMU as a PCI device. ARM platforms expose the SYSMMU via memory-mapped I/O regions. A VM on top of the hypervisor may perform direct IO to these devices, effectively compromising the integrity of the hypervisor. Therefore, an integrity-protected hypervisor *must* prevent access to these critical system devices at all times.

4.3 Design Rule

A hypervisor's runtime integrity can be compromised by manipulating its memory regions. On both x86 and ARM hardware virtualized platform memory can be accessed either via code executing on the CPU or system devices using DMA. In this section, we discuss the rule governing the design of an integrity-protected hypervisor in the above context.

Rule An integrity-protected hypervisors' code **must** be free of vulnerabilities.   □

Discussion: A hypervisor needs to be configured with guest environment state (guest OS and allocated resources) before a guest environment can be run. Furthermore, contingent on hypervisor design, configuration changes can be needed at runtime during guest environment operation (e.g., adding or removing resources at runtime). Depending on the hypervisor design, inter-VM communication (e.g., drag and drop between different guest environments) and guest runtime interfaces to the hypervisor (e.g., accelerated IO drivers for virtualized devices) might be supported. Such runtime interfaces might also directly access hypervisor data (e.g., accelerated drivers within the guest may access temporary data buffers that are mapped within hypervisor memory regions for fast IO). All these configuration options and interfaces pose significant risk to hypervisor integrity if they are complex (CVE, 2008). An integrity-protected hypervisor must therefore ensure that such configuration and runtime interfaces are minimal. Furthermore, designers must also ensure that the hypervisor's core operating logic is simple and its codebase is within limits to perform manual and analytical audits to rule out any vulnerabilities (Datta et al., 2009; Franklin et al., 2008; Klein et al., 2009).

References

Advanced (2005) AMD64 virtualization: secure virtual machine architecture reference manual. AMD Publication no. 33047 rev. 3.01

Anderson JP (1972) Computer security technology planning study. Tech. Rep. ESD-TR-73-51, Air Force Electronic Systems Division, Hanscom AFB

ARM Limited (2003) ARM builds security foundation for future wireless and consumer devices. ARM Press Release

ARM Limited (2009) ARM security technology: building a secure system using TrustZone technology. White Paper PRD29-GENC-009492C

ARM Limited (2010a) AMBA 4 AXI4-Stream protocol version 1.0 specification

ARM Limited (2010b) AMBA APB protocol version 2.0 specification

ARM Limited (2010c) Virtualization extensions architecture specification. http://infocenter.arm. com

Boileau A (2006) Hit by a bus: physical access attacks with FireWire. RuxCon

Budruk R, Anderson D, Shanley T (2004) PCI express system architecture. Addison-Wesley, Boston

CVE (2008) Directory traversal vulnerability in the shared folders feature. CVE-2008-0923 (under review)

Datta A, Franklin J, Garg D, Kaynar D (2009) A logic of secure systems and its applications to trusted computing. In: Proceedings of IEEE symposium on security and privacy

Duflot L, Levillain O, Morin B, Grumelard O (2009) Getting into the SMRAM: SMM reloaded. Central Directorate for Information Systems Security

Franklin J, Seshadri A, Qu N, Chaki S, Datta A (2008) Attacking, repairing, and verifying SecVisor: a retrospective on the security of a hypervisor. CMU CyLab Technical Report CMU-CyLab-08-008

Heasman J (2006a) Implementing and detecting a PCI rootkit. NGSSoftware Insight Security Research

Heasman J (2006b) Implementing and detecting an ACPI BIOS rootkit, Black Hat, USA

Heasman J (2007) Hacking the extensible firmware interface, Black Hat, USA

Hewlett-Packard et al (2006) Advanced configuration and power interface specification. Revision 3.0b

Intel (2005) Intel virtualization technology specification for the IA-32 Intel architecture. Intel Publication no. C97063-002

Intel Corporation (2002) The extensible firmware interface specification. http://www.intel.com/ technology/efi/

Kauer B (2007) OSLO: improving the security of trusted computing. In: Proceedings USENIX security symposium

Klein G, Elphinstone K, Heiser G, Andronick J, Cock D, Derrin P, Elkaduwe D, Engelhardt K, Kolanski R, Norrish M, Sewell T, Tuch H, Winwood S (2009) seL4: formal verification of an OS kernel. In: Proceedings SOSP

Popek GJ, Goldberg RP (1974) Formal requirements for virtualizable third generation architectures. Commun ACM 17(7):412–421

Robin JS, Irvine CE (2000) Analysis of the Intel Pentium's ability to support a secure virtual machine monitor. In: Proceedings USENIX security symposium

Rutkowska J (2006) Subverting Vista kernel for fun and profit. SyScan and Black Hat Presentations

Sacco AL, Ortega AA (2009) Persistent BIOS infection. Core Security Technologies

Saltzer J, Schroeder M (1975) The protection of information in computer systems. Proc IEEE 63(9):1278–1308

SecuriTeam (2004) Opteron exposed: reverse engineering AMD K8 microcode updates. SecuriTeam security reviews

Seshadri A, Luk M, Shi E, Perrig A, VanDoorn L, Khosla P (2005) Pioneer: verifying integrity and guaranteeing execution of code on legacy platforms. In: Proceedings SOSP

Shanley T, Anderson D (1999) PCI System Architecture. Addison-Wesley, Boston

Technologies P (2009) Phoenix SecureCore. http://www.phoenix.com

Trusted Computing Group (2007) Trusted platform module main specification. Version 1.2, Revision 103

Wojtczuk R, Rutkowska J (2008) Xen 0wning trilogy. Invisible Things Lab

Wojtczuk R, Rutkowska J (2009) Attacking SMM memory via Intel CPU cache poisoning. Invisible Things Lab

The Uber eXtensible Micro-Hypervisor Framework (UBERXMHF)

Abstract This chapter presents the uber eXtensible Micro-Hypervisor Framework (UBERXMHF), a micro-hypervisor architecture and framework that focuses on three goals which are keys to achieving practical security on commodity platforms: (a) commodity compatibility (e.g., runs unmodified Linux and Windows) and unfettered access to platform hardware; (b) efficient implementation; and (c) low trusted computing base and complexity. UBERXMHF strives to be a comprehensible, practical, and flexible platform for performing micro-hypervisor research and development. UBERXMHF encapsulates common hypervisor core functionality in a framework that allows developers and users to build custom micro-hypervisor-based solutions (called "uberapps") while freeing them from a considerable amount of wheel-reinventing that is often associated with such efforts. We are encouraged by the end result—a clean, bare-bones, open-source micro-hypervisor framework with desirable performance characteristics and an architecture amenable to formal analysis. Open-source development continues at: https://uberxmhf.org.

1 Introduction

Recent years have yielded significant research on hypervisor-based architectures for security (Vasudevan et al., 2012; Wang et al., 2012; Zhang et al., 2011; Vasudevan et al., 2011; McCune et al., 2010; Wang and Jiang, 2010; Fattori et al., 2010; Litty et al., 2008; Seshadri et al., 2007; Xiong et al., 2011; Singaravelu et al., 2006; Ben-Yehuda et al., 2010; Ta-Min et al., 2006; Dinaburg et al., 2008; Quist et al., 2011; Sharif et al., 2009). A majority of these hypervisors (Vasudevan et al., 2012; Wang et al., 2012; Zhang et al., 2011; Vasudevan et al., 2011; McCune et al., 2010; Wang and Jiang, 2010; Fattori et al., 2010; Litty et al., 2008; Seshadri et al., 2007) are designed and written from scratch with the primary goal of achieving a low Trusted Computing Base (TCB) while providing a specific security property. Other research efforts leverage existing commercial-grade virtualization solutions (e.g., Xen, Linux KVM, VMware, or L4), but generally do not require such rich functionality (Xiong et al., 2011; Singaravelu et al., 2006; Ben-Yehuda et al., 2010; Ta-Min et al., 2006;

Dinaburg et al., 2008; Quist et al., 2011; Sharif et al., 2009; Garfinkel et al., 2003; Chen et al., 2008).

This chapter discusses our efforts in developing UBERXMHF, an uber eXtensible Micro-Hypervisor Framework. UBERXMHF takes a *developer-centric* approach to micro-hypervisor design and implementation, and strives to be a comprehensible and flexible platform for performing micro-hypervisor research and development. We are motivated in part by the fact that every micro-hypervisor-based solution relies on a common core functionality that is inevitable when given a particular CPU architecture (e.g., x86, ARM). UBERXMHF encapsulates this common functionality in a framework that allows others to build custom micro-hypervisor-based solutions while freeing them from a considerable amount of (low-level, challenging to debug) wheel-reinventing that is often associated with such efforts.

We have ported a number of hypervisor research efforts to this new platform, essentially realizing a "version 2.0" implementation where development continues today. In this paper, we describe the design and implementation of UBERXMHF, emphasizing those design decisions which we feel are suitable for supporting modular development of future "micro-hypervisor assisted applications" or "uberapps." We describe several uberapps in the next chapter.

UBERXMHF advocates a "rich" single-guest model where the micro-hypervisor framework supports only a single-guest and allows the guest direct access to all performance-critical system devices and device interrupts. The single-guest model results in a dramatically reduced hypervisor complexity (since all devices are directly controlled by the OS) and consequently TCB, while at the same time promising near-native guest performance. In principle, the single-guest could also be another traditional hypervisor (e.g., Xen, KVM) which in turn supports multiple guests.

A uberapp relies on UBERXMHF for core platform functionality while extending the framework to implement a customized solution. As a small piece of software between the OS and the hardware, uberapps therefore enjoy a unique advantage in terms of balance between security and versatility. They also help reduce security sensitive developers concerns with respect to other malicious applications with the OS or OS vulnerabilities.

UBERXMHF currently supports both x86 (Intel and AMD) and ARM hardware virtualized platforms and can run Linux, Windows XP, and Windows 2003 as unmodified guests with SMP support. UBERXMHF imposes less than 10% overhead in the common case, and the current implementation as of this writing has a TCB of 6–13K SLoC depending on the extent of framework features used by an uberapp.

We are encouraged by the end result—a clean, bare-bones hypervisor framework with desirable performance characteristics and an architecture amenable to formal analysis. UBERXMHF is open-source and is available at: https://uberxmhf.org

2 Goals, Properties, and Assumptions

2.1 Goals

Our overarching goal is to enable design and development of performant security oriented applications on commodity platforms and to inject security properties in the existing platform and software stack. Our design goals fall broadly in three categories.

2.1.1 Commodity Compatibility and Unfettered Development

The micro-hypervisor design must integrate into the existing deployment ecosystem of commodity platforms. It must be able to run unmodified stock operating systems and kernels (e.g., Linux and Windows) and allow access to all programmable system peripherals (e.g., GPIO, I2C, SPI, USB, etc.). It must be generic enough to allow for a wide variety of security applications to be constructed. Finally, the development techniques must foster wider adoption by the already huge development base and prominent programming languages and development tools (e.g., C/Assembly).

2.1.2 Performance

Our solution must not preclude aggressive code optimization and must not adversely affect runtime performance. Furthermore, commodity OS on multi-core hardware must be supported.

2.1.3 Low TCB and Low Complexity

Our solution should have a low TCB and complexity to facilitate manual audits and/or formal verification. Recent advances in formal verification have shown this is a critical requirement for verifiability (Vasudevan et al., 2016; Gu et al., 2015).

2.2 System Properties and Applications

The UBERXMHF architecture provides the following fundamental system security guarantees (Fig. 1): (1) uberguest memory isolation and memory integrity of μHV and uberapps; (2) μHV and uberapps liveness; (3) μHV and uberapps memory protection from malicious system peripherals; and (4) secure boot. Chapter

System Properties	Architecture Mechanisms
1. Memory Integrity of μHV and uberapps	Memory Isolation
2. μHV and uberapps Liveness	Peripheral and Interrupt Partitioning
3. μHV and uberapps DMA protection	Trap-Intercept-Forward
4. Secure Boot	Trap-Intercept-Forward

Fig. 1 UBERXMHF system properties and high-level architecture mechanisms

"Micro-Hypervisor Applications" describes several uberapps that leverage these foundational system properties to realize a wide spectrum of security applications.

2.3 Non-goals

We focus on supporting a single OS which is the typical end-user usage model. We do not aim to run multiple operating systems or virtualize system resources in the traditional manner directly within the micro-hypervisor.

2.4 Attacker Model and Assumptions

We assume that the attacker does not have physical access to the commodity platform. The hardware TCB includes the CPU and supporting chipset including the memory controller. Other system peripherals and the OS kernel and applications are under the attacker's control. This is a reasonable assumption since a majority of attacks are mounted by malicious software or untrusted add-on boards interfacing via system peripherals. We assume that our hardware TCB is functionally correct.

3 Design

We design UBERXMHF as a Type-1 (or native, bare metal) hypervisor that runs directly on the host's hardware to control the hardware and to manage guest operating systems. A guest operating system thus runs on another (deprivileged) level above the hypervisor. Our primary design choice for a bare-metal hypervisor is for a low-TCB and high performance hypervisor code base. Figure 2 shows the high-level design of UBERXMHF. The UBERXMHF framework consists of the UBERXMHF core and supporting libraries that sit directly on top of the platform hardware. A uberapp extends UBERXMHF and leverages the basic hypervisor and platform functionality provided by the UBERXMHF core while implementing the desired (security) functionality.

3.1 "Rich" Single-Guest Execution Model

We propose a "rich" single-guest execution model where the hypervisor framework supports only a single-guest and—following UBERXMHF initialization—allows the guest direct access to all performance-critical system devices and device interrupts. We note that the single-guest execution model resonates with a plethora of recent works (Vasudevan et al., 2012; Wang et al., 2012; Zhang et al., 2011; Vasudevan et al., 2011; McCune et al., 2010; Wang and Jiang, 2010; Fattori et al., 2010; Litty et al., 2008; Seshadri et al., 2007) that attempt to provide desired functionality and security properties in the context of a single commodity operating environment. Note that the single-guest model allows its guest to be another (more traditional) hypervisor running multiple guest OSes, as evidenced by recent research efforts such as Cloudvisor (Zhang et al., 2011) and Turtles (Ben-Yehuda et al., 2010).

The "rich" single-guest model (see Fig. 2) has several advantages over traditional hypervisor approaches.

3.1.1 Dramatically Reduced Hypervisor Complexity and Consequently TCB

Since all devices are directly controlled by the guest, UBERXMHF does not have to deal with per-device idiosyncrasies that arise from devices that are not completely standards-compliant. Furthermore, UBERXMHF does not need to perform hardware multiplexing, an inherently complex mechanism that can lead to security issues (Karger and Safford, 2008; Elhage, 2011). This results in a small and simple hypervisor code base which improves maintainability and makes it amenable to formal verification and/or manual audits to rule out the incidence of vulnerabilities. Note that we could attempt to reduce device multiplexing by employing device-passthrough, where a device is directly assigned to a guest (Xen, 2011a). Unfortunately, the devices that can be allocated using this scheme depend directly on the platform bus hierarchy in a particular system (Xen, 2011c). Furthermore, device-passthrough support is not seamless currently and requires non-trivial device firmware extraction and patching in some cases (Xen, 2011b).

3.1.2 Narrow Attacker Interface

With the "rich" single-guest execution model, the hypervisor interacts with the guest via a deterministic and well-defined platform interface. For example, current x86 and ARM hardware virtualized platforms define a small deterministic set of *intercepts* that transfer control to the hypervisor upon detecting certain guest conditions. This greatly reduces the attack surface of UBERXMHF and the uberapp.

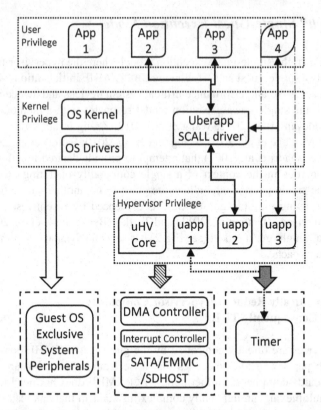

Fig. 2 UBERXMHF *micro-hypervisor-based system security architecture. Dashed boxes indicate logical peripheral groups; dotted boxes indicate operating privilege levels (user, kernel, hypervisor); dashed dotted box indicates a regular application split and bound to an exclusive uberapp; thick solid down-arrow indicates exclusive peripheral access by the* UBERXMHF *framework; hollow down-arrow indicates exclusive peripheral access by the uberguest; patterned down-arrow indicates peripheral accesses that are subject to trap-inspect-forward; solid bi-directional thin arrows indicate synchronous uberapp calls; dotted bi-directional thin arrow indicates asynchronous uberapp calls*

3.1.3 Near-Native Guest Performance

The system interrupt controllers (e.g., IOAPICs, GIC) and devices are directly in the control of the guest. Therefore, all (device) interrupts are configured and handled by the guest without the intervention of UBERXMHF. This results in a near-native guest performance (the guest still has to incur the memory/DMA protection overheads which are minimal in practice (Vasudevan et al., 2013; Vasudevan and Chaki, 2018)). This is in contrast to traditional hypervisors where the hypervisor virtualizes devices and interposes on all device interrupts. Note that even with device-passthrough, where a device can be directly assigned to a guest, the interrupts still need to be handled by the hypervisor resulting in noticeable performance degradation in practice (Gordon et al., 2012).

3.2 Architecture Overview

The high-level UBERXMHF system architecture (Fig. 2) is based on three core concepts: (a) μHV core and uberguest: most system peripherals are controlled directly by a single, commodity, unmodified OS (uberguest) achieving high performance while still ensuring strong isolation and runtime protection; (b) uberapps: act in the context of the uberguest or uberguest applications to provide required security properties; (c) μHV Trap-Inspect-Forward: facilitates secure boot and runtime protection of the μHV core and uberapps via light-weight peripheral and memory access interceptions.

3.3 μHV Core and Uberguest

The μHV core forms the heart of the UBERXMHF architecture and includes supporting libraries that sit directly on top of the platform hardware. The design choice of the uberguest being a single full-featured commodity unmodified OS fits squarely with the typical end-user usage scenario of a commodity platform and development ecosystem. This choice also allows us to greatly minimize μHV core complexity and consequently TCB since most system peripherals are directly handled by the uberguest. Furthermore, the uberguest model results in high performance since all peripheral interrupts are directly handled and serviced by the OS without any μHV core intervention. Sections 5 and 6 describe the uberguest implementation in more detail, along with challenges of handling guest memory reporting and multi-core enablement.

3.4 Uberguest Isolation

As UBERXMHF allows (in the common case) the guest to directly access system devices and handle interrupts, it must isolate itself from the guest in order to preserve its integrity—a fundamental hypervisor property. Integrity means that all changes to hypervisor memory are caused by direct action within the intended execution of the hypervisor's own instructions (e.g., initialization and intercept handlers). Furthermore, integrity requires that neither hypervisor code nor data can be directly accessed via Direct Memory Accesses (DMA) by devices. Consequently, UBERXMHF must ensure that it starts up in an unmodified fashion and continues to run without any inadvertent modifications to its code and data. We discuss below how UBERXMHF achieves runtime memory isolation of the uberguest from the micro-hypervisor framework. We discuss secure startup in Sect. 3.8.

As UBERXMHF allows the guest direct access to system devices, intuitively memory protection from devices and guest code (running on the CPU) becomes crucial to preserving its integrity and enforcing isolation.

Devices such as USB, FireWire, Storage and Network devices can directly access physical memory via DMA, potentially bypassing the hypervisor. These devices can be programmed by an attacker to access any portion of the physical memory including those belonging to the hypervisor (Boileau, 2006). Malicious firmware on a device can also accomplish the same goal by replacing legitimate physical memory addresses passed to it with hypervisor physical memory regions.

UBERXMHF leverages the platform I/O Memory Management Unit (IOMMU) protect its memory regions from direct access by devices. The IOMMU is the only system device that can intervene between DMA transactions occurring between a device and memory. Both AMD and Intel x86 platforms provide an IOMMU as a part of the northbridge. ARM server class platforms provide an IOMMU as part of the system MMU. On systems that lack an IOMMU (e.g., some ARM platforms) UBERXMHF employs trap-inspect-forward(Sect. 3.7) on the system DMA controllers to achieve the same effect.

The IOMMU allows each peripheral device in the system to be assigned to a set of IO page-tables. When an IO device attempts to access system memory, the IOMMU intercepts the access and uses the IO page-tables associated with that device to determine whether the access is to be permitted as well as the actual location in system memory that is to be accessed. UBERXMHF instantiates IO page-tables such that physical addresses corresponding to UBERXMHF memory regions are marked as inaccessible to any device.

A guest environment running on top of UBERXMHF can run any commodity OS and applications. The guest may manipulate the CPU MMU's virtual memory data structures or even directly access system physical memory belonging to the hypervisor. UBERXMHF uses *partitions*[1] to contain guest code and data. Partitions in UBERXMHF are essentially bare-bones CPU hardware backed execution containers which enforce system memory isolation for the guest or a portion of it.

UBERXMHF creates a primary partition in order to run the guest operating environment. The primary partition allows the guest environment to see and access all the system devices including the CPU (and cores) just as it would have on a native boot. UBERXMHF can also instantiate secondary partitions on demand when requested by a uberapp. These secondary partitions are capable of running portions of the guest environment code/data within isolation (Fig. 2). This is useful when a uberapp wishes to implement desired security properties at a finer-granularity of portions of an untrusted application within the operating environment (e.g., TrustVisor (McCune et al., 2010))

UBERXMHF leverages hardware virtualization second-stage page-tables for uberguest memory isolation. The second-stage page-tables are resident within the μHV core memory regions and ensure that uberguest physical memory accesses are translated to the actual system physical address via a hardware second-stage page-walk. The UBERXMHF memory regions are marked inaccessible within the

---

[1] The term hardware virtual machine is used for such CPU execution containers in current hardware virtualization parlance. However, technically a virtual machine presents to the guest a virtualized view of the system devices in addition to enforcing memory isolation, and is a misnomer in our case.

second-stage page-tables which will cause the hardware to disallow any direct memory access to the UBERXMHF memory regions by the uberguest.

3.4.1 μHV Core Peripheral and Interrupt Partitioning

Certain security applications may entail reserving specific system peripherals for exclusive use by the μHV core and/or the uberapps and the subsequent handling and servicing of their interrupts, e.g., a dedicated system timer for secure periodic processing.

UBERXMHF handles such peripheral mappings using the hardware second-stage page-tables described previously, to ensure that the uberguest does not see or have unrestricted access to the peripheral that is reserved for (exclusive) use by UBERXMHF.

On commodity platforms which allow hardware interrupt virtualization (e.g., certain x86 and ARM hardware virtualized platforms), UBERXMHF uses hardware interrupt redirection (e.g., vGIC, vAPIC) in order to route appropriate device interrupts to the corresponding partition. However, partitioning interrupts on commodity platforms without hardware support is more challenging.

UBERXMHF leverages some key platform insights to allow interrupt partitioning without dedicated interrupt virtualization hardware and complex peripheral emulation on both commodity x86 and ARM platforms.

On commodity x86 platforms every interrupt is routed via an Interrupt Descriptor Table (IDT) which is an area of memory usually under the control of the uberguest. Every interrupt has a corresponding handler address within the IDT. For a device under exclusive control of a partition, UBERXMHF redirects the corresponding device interrupt vector to the partition via a hypercall. Furthermore, it marks the IDT read-only to ensure that such interrupt redirections cannot be compromised by the untrusted uberguest.

On commodity ARM architectures, UBERXMHF uses a similar mechanism for interrupt redirection. ARM architectures support two overarching interrupt mechanisms (fast and regular), but commodity OSes only make use of regular interrupt mechanism. Second, ARM platforms regular interrupt controllers allow programming of a particular device interrupt to use either the fast or regular interrupt mechanism. UBERXMHF therefore programs the interrupt controller to use fast interrupts for devices that are exclusively held by partitions. UBERXMHF then intercepts the fast interrupts via hardware virtualization primitives and routes the interrupt to the appropriate partition.

3.5 Uberapps and Uberapp Interactions

Just like a regular application running inside an operating system accesses services via a plethora of interfaces (kernel, windowing, graphics, shell, etc.), UBERXMHF and uberapps interact with a guest operating system via an event-based interface during runtime. However, unlike regular application interfaces, this event-based interface is extremely small with well-defined CPU populated parameters, thereby greatly reducing the attack surface of UBERXMHF and the uberapp. At the same time, this interface is versatile enough to realize several practical security applications as evidenced by several recent efforts (Vasudevan et al., 2012; Wang et al., 2012; Zhang et al., 2011; Vasudevan et al., 2011; McCune et al., 2010; Wang and Jiang, 2010; Fattori et al., 2010; Litty et al., 2008; Seshadri et al., 2007; Xiong et al., 2011; Singaravelu et al., 2006; Ben-Yehuda et al., 2010; Ta-Min et al., 2006; Dinaburg et al., 2008; Quist et al., 2011; Sharif et al., 2009).

UBERXMHF leverages CPU support for hardware virtualization in order to capture and handle events within a guest operating environment. For example, current x86 hardware virtualized platforms define a deterministic set of *intercepts* that transfer control to the hypervisor upon detecting certain guest conditions. This includes nested page fault, I/O port traps, instruction traps, exception traps, and hypercalls. Similar capabilities are also available on hardware-virtualized ARM processors (ARM Limited, 2010). In UBERXMHF these interactions are serviced by the μHV core (e.g., guest memory reporting) or handled by a μHV core extension that we term uberapps. UBERXMHF during initialization allows a uberapp to configure the set of guest events that it wishes to intercept and handle. This avoids unnecessary guest intercepts at runtime.

The μHV core gets control for all intercepted guest events and in turn invokes the appropriate UBERXMHF/uberapp *callback* to handle the event. The UBERXMHF/uberapp *callback* has the option of injecting the event back into the guest for further processing if desired. The event-callback mechanism therefore allows uberapps to easily *extend* core UBERXMHF functionality to realize desired functionality in the context of a particular guest. For example, tracking uberguest process contexts for application privacy or a watchdog application for ensuring keep-alive sensitive operations in the face uberguest failures or breach.

UBERXMHF also advocates a development ecosystem where a regular uberguest application can have its sensitive portions isolated as uberapps which are isolated from the remainder of the uberguest and other applications. For example, storing sensitive signing keys for an encrypted filesystem or for platform attestation.

Uberapps can be synchronous (e.g., invoked via a synchronous call; SCALL) or asynchronous (e.g., executed periodically). UBERXMHF uses a combination of hardware virtualization traps and architecture physical timers to support both uberapp execution models. This allows for a wide range of security applications to be developed in practice. We discuss some of these applications in the next chapter.

3.6 Attested Measurements

Remotely ascertaining the cryptographic hash of executable code is commonly achieved via an attestation protocol. Such protocols generate a cryptographically signed or otherwise authenticated message containing one or more digests of the target executable code. We distinguish two facets of an attestation protocol: (1) accumulating measurements on the target system of interest, and (2) verifying the attested measurements on a trusted verifier system.

UBERXMHF relies on a Trusted Platform Module (TPM) for accumulating integrity measurements. The TPM could be a hardware module (e.g., in most commodity x86 platforms and some ARM platforms) or a software module (e.g., on commodity platforms lacking hardware support). TPMs contain Platform Configuration Registers (PCRs), which are registers that store an append-only hash chain.

Using either dynamic root of trust or static root of trust as part of the launch process (see Sect. 3.8), the hash of the code being launched is extended into a PCR. This PCR can be extended further as components are loaded and executed.

A challenge with this approach is that monitoring a PCR value for changes does not reveal any insight into the reason for a change. To be meaningful, remote attestations require a TCB that is relatively small and modular. It is then easier to keep track of a list of known-good components, and the micro-hypervisor is presumed to be less susceptible to runtime compromise (due to its lower complexity/small size). This is important because the attestation is a load-time property (i.e., it only tells the verifier what code was loaded). Attestation cannot detect if a runtime exploit overwrites loaded code with unauthorized code.

UBERXMHF addresses this problem by having a modular approach to its design. Every component of the core and supporting libraries can be essentially considered as objects exposing a set of interfaces and dealing with object data. Every UBERXMHF component and the uberapp have the following memory layout: code, init-data, uninitialized-data, and stack (if applicable). During load, the code and init-data are hashed and extended into a PCR for attestation purposes, while the uninitialized-data and stack are zeroed out to begin with.

3.7 Protections via Trap-Inspect-Forward

UBERXMHF uses hardware second-stage page-table protections and hardware virtualization traps for light-weight trap-inspect-forward (TIF) where peripheral accesses are selectively *trapped* and *inspected* for correct accesses before *forwarding* the access directly to the physical system peripheral. UBERXMHF TIF allows implementing various system protections without resorting to complex peripheral .emulation and state maintenance. In practice, TIF results in low-TCB and incurs minimal performance overhead (Vasudevan et al., 2013; Vasudevan and Chaki, 2018). We discuss below two typical use-cases for TIF that allow DMA protections and interrupt protections on platforms without corresponding hardware support (e.g., IOMMU or Interrupt Redirection).

3.7.1 DMA Protection

A malicious guest or system peripheral can mount DMA style attacks (Rushanan and Checkoway, 2015) in order to compromise UBERXMHF memory integrity. On systems without hardware support for DMA protection, UBERXMHF employs TIF on the legacy DMA controller register space to prevent any form of DMA attacks in the system. Further details on how this is achieved in the context of a low-cost platform such as Raspberry PI can be found in Vasudevan and Chaki (2018).

3.7.2 Interrupt Protection

A buggy or malicious guest can tamper with a legacy interrupt controller to disable certain interrupt classes or routing mechanisms resulting in denial of service type attacks. UBERXMHF leverages TIF to protect the legacy interrupt controller register space to preserve interrupt routings setup by the UBERXMHF μHV core and/or uberapps.

3.8 Secure Boot

UBERXMHF loads itself during the platform initialization and boot sequence. For UBERXMHF to startup in an unmodified form entails trusting the platform initialization and boot sequence to correctly load and transfer control to UBERXMHF. Unfortunately ensuring this is a challenge on commodity x86 and ARM platforms. For example, malware in the uberguest can tamper with the binary images on the boot-partition to subvert subsequent loading of the framework. Secure boot is one such mechanism to prevent such attacks on commodity platforms and ensure load-time integrity.

3.8.1 Secure Boot via Dynamic Root-of-Trust

Traditional x86 BIOS initialization and boot sequence is plagued by having existed for several decades. As such, modern security requirements and virtualization capabilities did not exist when it was first conceived. The result of this is that there may exist legacy code in a system's BIOS, option ROMs and boot-sequence that should not be trusted, since it was never subjected to rigorous analysis for security issues.[2]

---

[2] A closed system where only known firmware is executed at boot-time, can be subjected to analysis and consequently trusted. However, most (if not all) x86 systems do not fall under this category.

UBERXMHF leverages dynamic root of trust (DRT) to startup in an unmodified fashion. A dynamic root of trust (DRT) is an execution environment created through a disruptive event that synchronizes and reinitializes all CPUs in the system to a known good state. It also disables all interrupt sources, DMA, and debugging access to the new environment. DRT support is available on all current commodity x86 CPUs from Intel and AMD (Intel Corporation, 2006; Advanced Micro Devices, 2005).

UBERXMHF's launch process consists of an initialization module that is loaded via a (untrusted) boot-loader such as GRUB. The initialization module then uses appropriate CPU instructions to establish a DRT and loads UBERXMHF in a memory constrained hardware protected environment. UBERXMHF in turn initializes the platform and sets up required protections to run the uberguest and uberapps with appropriate access to platform resources.

3.8.2 Secure Boot via Static Root-of-Trust

On platforms that do not contain support for dynamic root-of-trust, UBERXMHF employs static root-of-trust to launch the framework in an unmodified fashion. UBERXMHF uses a combination of trusted deployment (see Sect. 4) and trap-inspect-forward (see Sect. 3.7) to achieve secure boot via a static root-of-trust.

The UBERXMHF lifecycle (see Sect. 4) ensures that a valid boot-partition image is in place to start with. This ensures that the integrity of the chain of execution to the UBERXMHF framework binary is valid to begin with. UBERXMHF enforces a key requirement towards preserving the integrity of the boot-partition contents. The boot-partition on a platform running UBERXMHF is of a fixed length and is exclusive to UBERXMHF (i.e., not required or used by the uberguest).

UBERXMHF takes advantage of the fact that the platform storage is typically managed by a host storage controller (e.g., SATA, AHCI, EMMC/SDHOST) which implements the required data transfer protocol and directs storage operations to the attached storage device (e.g., hard-disk, SD card). When the uberguest writes to the host storage controller registers for read and write operations, UBERXMHF intercepts only the write operations and inspects the storage controller registers to ensure that the target sector addresses do not belong to the boot-partition. If it does, it denies the write. In practice, such interpositioning has minimal effect on the system performance (Vasudevan and Chaki, 2018; Vasudevan et al., 2012). Figure 3 shows an example of how UBERXMHF achieves secure-boot via static root-of-trust on a low-cost platform such as Raspberry PI.

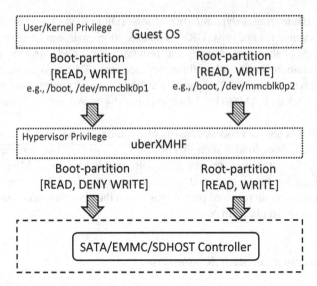

Fig. 3 UBERXMHF secure boot leverages intercept and inspect mechanism (indicated by Patterned down-arrow) on the MMC and SDHOST controller in order to deny writes to the boot-partition containing UBERXMHF boot binaries while passing through all other accesses

4 UBERXMHF Lifecycle

4.1 Installation

End-users receive the UBERXMHF pre-loaded with the boot-partition image from the UBERXMHF distributor (described later in this section). System developers on the other hand can receive the UBERXMHF installation kit, consisting of a signed boot-partition image from the UBERXMHF distributor, which they verify using the public key and copy it to the boot-partition of the target platform. Then the user optionally (re-)configures the UBERXMHF μHV core and uberapps, e.g., compile a custom binary image with required uberapps from a signed source blob. UBERXMHF is now ready for startup and normal operation.

4.2 Startup and Recovery

On bootup UBERXMHF μHV core is loaded which in turn initializes the uberapps and eventually boots the uberguest. Normal system operation is characterized by uberguest execution interspersed with μHV core and uberapp interactions. When the uberguest is shutdown, the UBERXMHF μHV core gets control and cleans up required internal state including those of uberapps before powering down the system. Malicious uberguest behavior (e.g., writing to UBERXMHF memory regions, performing DMA to UBERXMHF memory regions, etc.) is disallowed gracefully by ignoring such actions. However, such actions can also be handled via a dedicated uberapp for required user signaling if required.

4.3 UBERXMHF *Distributor*

The role of the UBERXMHF distributor might be played by a trusted company or organization (e.g., IBM, Microsoft, Google). UBERXMHF's key insight is that by agreeing to install and use UBERXMHF, the user is expressing their trust in the UBERXMHF distributor, since UBERXMHF will be operating with maximum privileges. To some extent, OS distributions today already implicitly operate on this assumption. When a user installs a distribution they also trust those distributions to provide software that does not contain malware.

4.4 *Updates*

As UBERXMHF components (μHV core and uberapps) evolve, they need to be updated. This process is straightforward since the UBERXMHF distributor can simply release a signed list of the update and/or source binary to be installed as described in the beginning of this section.

5 UBERXMHF Implementation on x86 Platforms

We now describe the UBERXMHF implementation on commodity x86 hardware virtualized platforms. The framework implementation supports both Intel and AMD and is capable of running unmodified legacy SMP capable Windows (2003 and XP) and Linux.

5.1 *Rich-Guest Execution Model*

5.1.1 Multi-Core Guest Boot-Up

Summary
A native operating system on the x86 platform uses the INIT and Startup Inter-Processor Interrupt (SIPI) in order to bring up multiple cores (Intel Corporation, 2005; Advanced Micro Devices, 2005). The INIT-SIPI-SIPI sequence is delivered to a CPU core via the CPU Local Advanced Programmable Interrupt Controller

(LAPIC). However, when a guest OS runs on top of UBERXMHF, the framework must ensure that it maintains required protections during runtime while allowing the guest OS to access the physical cores directly. Normal hypervisors such as Xen virtualize the CPU LAPIC in order to handle SMP guests. This results in considerable code complexity as a result of handling issues such as concurrency and interrupt ordering. In contrast, UBERXMHF allows the guest direct access to the LAPIC. Therefore, ensuring that the framework is still able to retain control and maintain isolation during runtime is a challenge.

Details

On a single core CPU, UBERXMHF during initialization switches the Boot Strap Processor (BSP) core to guest-mode before booting the guest OS. For a multi-core CPU, UBERXMHF during initialization activates the remaining cores in the system and switches them to host-mode which then idle within UBERXMHF. When the guest initiates the INIT and SIPI sequence in order to bring up multiple cores, UBERXMHF intercepts this sequence and switches the cores to guest-mode before handing back execution to the guest.

To support both Intel and AMD x86 platforms, UBERXMHF uses a generic scheme to intercept guest multi-core activation. The LAPIC Interrupt Control Register (ICR) is used to deliver the INIT-SIPI-SIPI sequence to a target core. On both Intel and AMD hardware-virtualized platforms, the LAPIC registers are accessed via memory-mapped I/O. The memory-mapped I/O region encompasses a single physical memory page. UBERXMHF leverages hardware page-tables to trap and intercept any changes to the LAPIC memory-mapped I/O page by the guest.

Subsequently, any writes to the LAPIC ICR by the guest causes the hardware to trigger an intercept. The UBERXMHF core handles this intercept, disables guest interrupts, and sets the guest *trap-flag* and resumes the guest. This causes the hardware to immediately trigger a single-step intercept, which is then handled by the UBERXMHF core to process the instruction that caused the write to the LAPIC ICR. If a INIT command was being written to the ICR, UBERXMHF simply voids the instruction. When the SIPI command is written to the ICR, UBERXMHF voids the instruction and instead runs the target guest code on that core in *guest-mode*.

5.1.2 Core Quiescing

Summary

In a multi-core system, the other cores need to be in a halted state when the UBERXMHF core or uberapp is modifying critical data structures such as the nested page-tables as this affects the way in which all cores perceive memory.

Detail

UBERXMHF uses a mechanism called *core quiescing* in order to stall all cores in a multi-core system within a uberapp. UBERXMHF leverages the Non-Maskable Interrupt (NMI) for core quiescing as described below. When a uberapp on a specific core C wants to perform quiescing it invokes the UBERXMHF core interface which sends a NMI to all cores other than C. Since the NMI cannot be masked, this causes all these other cores to either receive a NMI intercept (if operating in guest mode) or a NMI exception (if operating in host mode). The NMI handler is invoked in both cases which is an idle spin-lock loop, in effect, stalling the core. Once the uberapp is done performing the required task on C, it signals the spin-lock which causes the other cores to resume.

5.1.3 Rich-Guest Memory Reporting

Summary
A normal guest operating system during its bootup uses the BIOS to determine the amount of physical memory in the system. More specifically the INT 15h E820 interrupt interface is the standard way of obtaining the system physical memory map from the BIOS. However, with a hypervisor loaded, there must be a mechanism to report a reduced memory map devoid of the hypervisor memory regions to the guest. If not, the guest at some point during its initialization will end up accessing the hypervisor memory areas. As described previously, a traditional hypervisor solution maps a virtual BIOS for a virtual machine which reports a reduced system memory map. However, this mechanism cannot be used for the "rich" single-guest model where the guest gets to see and interact with the real system BIOS.

Detail
UBERXMHF leverages the hardware page-tables for the purpose of reporting a custom system memory map to the guest OS. During initialization UBERXMHF locates the INT 15h interrupt handler address by scanning the real-mode Interrupt Vector Table (IVT). It then replaces the physical page entry corresponding to the interrupt handler in the nested page table to point to a buffer within UBERXMHF. This buffer is an exact copy of the original interrupt handler page with the starting of the INT 15h handler replaced by a hypercall instruction. When the guest OS invokes the INT 15h service during system bootup, the hypercall instruction transfers control to UBERXMHF which then checks to see if is it a memory map request. If so, it presents a custom memory map devoid of UBERXMHF memory regions and resumes the guest. If not, it injects the interrupt back to the guest for further processing.

5.2 μHV Core and Uberguest

The UBERXMHF μHV core performs the following operations: (a) initializes μHV nested-page-tables (NPT) and extended page-tables (EPT) and the uberguest virtual machine control block (VMCB) and virtual machine control structures (VMCS) on the AMD and Intel x86 hardware virtualized platforms, respectively; (b) sets up memory protections via NPTs and EPTS; (c) sets up DMA protection using the IOMMU; (d) sets up interrupt and boot protections; and (c) transfers control to the uberguest kernel to start the OS boot process.

5.3   Uberguest Isolation

5.3.1   Memory Isolation

UBERXMHF uses two-level Hardware Page-Tables (HPT)[3] for efficient memory isolation. In particular, the hardware ensures that all memory accesses by guest instructions go via a two-level translation in the presence of the HPT. First, the virtual address supplied by the guest is translated to a guest physical addresses using guest paging structures. Next, the guest physical addresses are translated into the actual system physical addresses using the permissions specified within the HPT. If the access requested by the guest violates the permissions stored in the HPT, the hardware triggers an intercept that can be handled by the UBERXMHF μHV core and/or the uberapp.

In UBERXMHF, both primary (where the guest OS runs) and secondary partitions (recall Sect. 3.4) are tied to a given HPT that enforces memory isolation. The partitions can all share the same HPT (for uniform view of memory and protections) or can have separate HPTs (cases where the secondary partition might want to run only with a subset of the primary partition address space).

5.3.2   Runtime DMA Protection

UBERXMHF *secure-loader* provides early DMA protection to the UBERXMHF runtime. However, this protection is very coarse grained (over a single contiguous range). To provide uberapps with a more flexible and fine-grained DMA protection capability, the UBERXMHF runtime reinitializes the DMA protection upon getting control. We now describe how fine-grained DMA protection is achieved on both AMD and Intel x86 platforms.

On AMD platforms, UBERXMHF relies on the DEV for fine-grained DMA protection. As discussed previously, DEV's bitmap structure allows DMA protection to be set at a page granularity. On Intel platforms, UBERXMHF uses the IOMMU page-tables in order to provide fine-grained page-level DMA protection. The IOMMU has a master table called the Root-Entry-Table (RET) which is 4 KB. Each 128-bit RET entry essentially corresponds to a PCI bus number (256 in total). Each

---

[3]Called Nested Page Tables on AMD and Extended Page-Table (EPT) on Intel Platforms, respectively.

RET entry points to a Context Entry Table (CET) which is 4 KB in size. Each 128-bit CET entry accounts for 32 devices with 8 functions per device as per the PCI specification. Each CET entry points to a regular PAE-page-table structure which contains mappings and protections for the DMA address space as seen by the device. Since UBERXMHF uses the "rich" single-guest model, all CET entries point to a single PAE-page-table structure that controls the DMA protections for all devices in the system.

5.3.3 μHV Core Peripheral and Interrupt Partitioning

System devices on commodity x86 platforms expose their interface through either legacy IO or memory-mapped IO. Normal hypervisors such as Xen use device virtualization to present to the guest, a different platform device configuration and I/O areas based on the guest configuration. However, since UBERXMHF lets the guest see and interact with the real system BIOS, it must employ a different mechanism to allocate peripherals to partitions.

UBERXMHF leverages hardware page-tables (EPTs or NPTs on Intel and AMD x86 platforms, respectively) for efficient peripheral memory configuration partitioning. For any given system device assigned to a particular partition, UBERXMHF maps all the memory configuration space assigned to the device to the corresponding partition's hardware page-table within the EPTs/NPTs. It also makes the memory-mapped I/O space of these devices inaccessible in other partitions' hardware page-tables. Furthermore, UBERXMHF uses hardware virtualization I/O intercepts to ensure that any other partition apart from the one having exclusive access to the device cannot perform legacy I/O.

5.4 Uberapps and Uberapp Interactions

5.4.1 Synchronous Uberapp Interactions

x86 hardware virtualization traps provide a hardware enforced mechanism for synchronous uberapp interactions. The VMCALL (on Intel x86) and VMMCALL (on AMD x86) instructions are used to perform a hypercall and are used as a primary means for synchronous uberapp interactions from the uberguest. Other synchronous uberapp interactions happen via hardware assisted trap mechanisms including second-stage page-faults (as a result of protection violation in the second-stage page-tables) and designated instruction traps (e.g., execution of system instructions). Upon all such traps, the μHV core gets control, marshals required parameters and transfers control to the corresponding uberapp handlers.

Event-class	Callback Prototype	Callback handled by
CPU Control register access	uxmhf_cb_handleCRaccess(vcpu, [CRparams...])	UBERXMHF core and uberapp
CPU Debug register access	uxmhf_cb_handleDRaccess(vcpu, [DRparams...])	UBERXMHF uberapp
CPU MSR access	uxmhf_cb_handleMSRaccess(vcpu, [MSRparams...])	UBERXMHF uberapp
CPU Exceptions	uxmhf_cb_handleEXCP(vcpu, [EXCPparams...])	UBERXMHF uberapp
Non-maskable Interrupt (NMI)	uxmhf_cb_handleNMI(vcpu, [NMIparams...])	UBERXMHF core
INIT/Shutdown	uxmhf_cb_handleINIT(vcpu, [INITparams...])	UBERXMHF core and uberapp
CPU Descriptor Table access	uxmhf_cb_handleXTRaccess(vcpu, [XTRparams...])	UBERXMHF uberapp
CPU Instructions	uxmhf_cb_handleINSN(vcpu, [INSNparams...])	UBERXMHF core and uberapp
Hypercall	uxmhf_cb_handleHYPC(vcpu, [HYPCparams...])	UBERXMHF uberapp
Legacy I/O access	uxmhf_cb_handleIOaccess(vcpu, [IOparams...])	UBERXMHF core and uberapp
CPU Task Switch	uxmhf_cb_handleTASK(vcpu, [TASKparams...])	UBERXMHF uberapp
CPU Nested Page Fault	uxmhf_cb_handleNPF(vcpu, [NPFparams...])	UBERXMHF core and uberapp

Fig. 4 UBERXMHF uses an event-callback approach to allow the uberapp to interact with the guest. An uberapp can configure the primary and/or the secondary partitions to intercept required guest events choosing from the broad event classes (example shown for AMD and Intel x86 platforms). For each event class, a uberapp callback is invoked in the corresponding CPU core context with associated parameters

5.4.2 Asynchronous Uberapp Interactions

The x86 Local Advanced Programmable Interrupt Controller (LAPIC) has support for per-core physical timers. The timer-value is the physical timer and is incremented every clock cycle. The control register is programmed to trigger an interrupt if it matches the compare value register, UBERXMHF programs the LAPIC to generate reserved interrupt which is then reflected to UBERXMHF via the interrupt descriptor table (IDT) via a hypercall (cf. Sect. 3.4.1). The hypercall handler within the μHV core is responsible for invoking the corresponding uberapp timer handler for any periodic processing.

5.4.3 Uberapp API

UBERXMHF uses an event-callback approach to allow the uberapp to interact with the guest and provide required capabilities. A uberapp can configure the primary and/or the secondary partitions to intercept required guest events choosing from the broad event classes on both AMD and Intel x86 platforms as shown in Fig. 4. For each intercepted class of event the UBERXMHF event-hub component invokes uberapp callback with the associated parameters in the context of the physical CPU core on which the intercept was triggered. For example, on a nested page fault, the uberapp gets the faulting virtual address, physical address, and the error code associated with the fault. Note that the UBERXMHF event-hub hides sub-architecture (AMD vs Intel) specific details and presents the hyperapp with a common architectural (x86) state. The uberapp callback is of course free to include sub-architecture specific handling as needed. The uberapp callback can choose to handle the event and/or inject it back to the guest for further processing. Also note from the figure that some events are also processed by the core directly, e.g., to handle core-quiescing (NMI intercept), shutdown (INIT/shutdown), and SMP guest bringup (INIT, DB exception, and nested page fault intercept).

5.5 Attested Measurements

We first summarize the memory layout of the UBERXMHF secure-loader and the UBERXMHF runtime. We then describe how hashes of various components are computed during the build process. Finally we describe how these hashes are then used to attest the launch of UBERXMHF and the uberapp to a local or remote verifier.

The memory layout of the UBERXMHF runtime components consist of the code, init-data, uninit-data, and stack as described previously in Sect. 3.6. The UBERXMHF secure-loader contains an extra region called .sl_untrusted_params which contains the untrusted input data for the secure-loader that is passed by UBERXMHF initialization module. This untrusted data is a secure-loader parameter block which contains boot time parameters that are used by the UBERXMHF core for platform initialization and configuration information that may be uberapp specific. The UBERXMHF secure-loader is responsible for validating all input data in the .sl_untrusted_params region. It is not measured by default, though a particular uberapp may measure anything it likes.

During the uberapp build process, the UBERXMHF runtime components and the UBERXMHF secure-loader are built and the expected ("golden") hash itself is computed from the UBERXMHF secure-loader and runtime binaries using a utility such as sha1sum. This "golden" hash can be used to compare the result of a platform attestation to convince a local or remote verifier that UBERXMHF and the uberapp executed on the platform. This process is further described in detail below.

The UBERXMHF secure-loader is measured by the CPU during creation of the DRT (i.e., SKINIT on AMD or GETSEC[SENTER] on Intel). The first 64K of the secure-loader is measured implicitly during DRTM establishment and stored in TPM PCRs 17 or 18 on AMD and Intel, respectively. Note that the expected measurement of the secure-loader will be different depending on whether it was launched on an Intel CPU or an AMD CPU due to Intel's requirement for an SINIT module and the differences in the secure-loader header as described previously. The secure-loader in turn hashes the UBERXMHF runtime and extends its measurement into PCR 17 (or 18). Thus, PCR 17 (or 18) will take on the value:
$H(H(0x00||H(secure-loader))||H(runtime))$. The properties of the hash function, TPM, chipset, and CPU guarantee that no other operation can cause PCR 17 (or 18) to take on this value. Thus, an attestation of the value of PCR 17 (or 18) will convince the verifier that UBERXMHF and the intended uberapp were launched on the target platform.

5.6   Protections via Trap-Inspect-Forward

5.6.1   Access-Control for Critical System Devices

Summary
Critical system devices such as the IOMMU and the system memory controller, like any other device expose their interface through either legacy IO or memory-mapped IO. For example, Intel x86 platforms expose the IOMMU as a DMA device through ACPI while AMD x86 platforms expose the DMA protection unit (DEV) as a PCI device. The system memory controller is typically exposed as a PCI device as well. With the "rich" single-guest model, the guest can perform direct I/O to these devices, effectively compromising the memory and DMA protections. Normal hypervisors such as Xen use a virtual BIOS to present to the guest a different platform device configuration and I/O areas and can easily mask platform critical devices from guest access. However, since UBERXMHF lets the guest see and interact with the real system BIOS, it must employ a different mechanism to prevent access to platform critical system devices.

Detail
UBERXMHF marks the ACPI and PCI configuration space of critical system devices (IOMMU, DEV, and system memory controller, for example) as *not-present* using the hardware page-tables. Thus, the guest never gets to see these devices in the first place. It also makes the memory-mapped I/O space of these devices inaccessible and sets intercepts on the legacy I/O space to prevent a guest from maliciously accessing these system devices.

5.6.2   TPM Sharing

UBERXMHF leverages the TPM for platform attestation. However, UBERXMHF also lets the guest environment see the physical TPM and communicate with it directly. Thus, UBERXMHF has to multiplex the TPM in a way so that both the guest and UBERXMHF and/or the uberapp can access the TPM functionality efficiently and without disruption. UBERXMHF leverages TPM localities for this purpose (Trusted Computing Group, 2007).

The TPM definition provides for localities or indications of specific platform processes. The TPM PC Specific Specification (Trusted Computing Group, 2005) defines five localities 0 through 4. A reserved set of page-aligned memory addresses correlates with the localities. Locality 4 is used by the hardware DRT mechanism and allows the TPM to respond appropriately to hardware DRT requests (i.e., SKINIT and GETSEC[SENTER]) for measurement and resetting of PCR. Locality 3 is provided for (optional) auxiliary components that may or may not be part of the hardware DRT process. UBERXMHF reserves locality 2 for the uberapp and also uses it to store the secure-loader and runtime measurements. UBERXMHF reserves localities 0 and 1 for use by the guest. Furthermore, UBERXMHF also masks locality 2 from the view of the guest using hardware page-tables to mark the corresponding locality 2 memory page as not-present. This restricts the guest to use only TPM locality 0 and 1 for its desired purpose. Note that for platforms where the TPM is implemented as a software-module, this sharing logic is part of the software TPM implementation which is protected from the untrusted uberguest via hardware page-table protections.

5.7 Secure Boot

UBERXMHF's init module is responsible for initiating a dynamic root of trust (DRT) in order to bootstrap the UBERXMHF secure-loader. DRT implementation has significant requirements on each of AMD and Intel x86 hardware platforms. We first briefly outline these requirements before proceeding to describe the UBERXMHF secure-loader implementation. AMD calls the launched environment a Secure-Loader Block (SLB). Intel calls the launched environment a Measured Launched Environment (MLE). For brevity we will use the term secure-loader.

UBERXMHF init
On AMD platforms, UBERXMHF init uses the SKINIT CPU instruction in order to establish a DRT and load the UBERXMHF secure-loader. As per SKINIT requirements, UBERXMHF init clears microcode on the BSP and all APs and ensures that the UBERXMHF secure-loader is loaded on a 64K-aligned physical address.

Intel platforms support DRT with their Trusted eXecution Technology (TXT). As part of TXT several MSRs are added to the CPU which are used to set up required data structures for DRT initialization and are also used for status and error reporting. TXT also requires a chipset specific Authenticated Code Module (also known as SINIT AC module) to establish a DRT. UBERXMHF init copies the appropriate SINIT AC module to the physical address specified by the TXT MSRs. The UBERXMHF init module then constructs page-tables that map the UBERXMHF secure-loader so that the SINIT AC module can address it properly. These page-tables are part of the UBERXMHF secure-loader memory.[4] The UBERXMHF init then sets up the CPU Memory Type Range Registers (MTRRs) in order to disable memory caching for the SINIT AC module to run. Finally, UBERXMHF init issues the GETSEC[SENTER] CPU instruction to establish a DRT and transfer control to the UBERXMHF secure-loader.

---

[4]In practice 3 4K pages should suffice. These are PAE-formatted page-tables.

UBERXMHF secure-loader

Both Intel and AMD differ in their SLB/MLE size constraints, CPU state when `secure-loader` gets control and layout of the `secure-loader`. AMD SLBs are limited to 64K in size while Intel MLEs can be larger. Intel and AMD SLB/MLEs both start in 32-bit flat protected mode, but have different CPU states. On AMD, only CS and SS are valid. EAX contains the SL base address and EDX contains the CPU information. ESP is initialized to top of 64K. On Intel, CS and DS are valid and SS is invalid and uninitialized.[5] Finally AMD SLBs and Intel MLEs have different header requirements.

UBERXMHF uses a single 64 KB `secure-loader` for both Intel and AMD platforms. The UBERXMHF `secure-loader` memory image starts with three empty pages, except for the first 4 bytes. These are initialized to contain the SLB header for an AMD system. The entry point points beyond these three pages to the true entry point on the fourth page. On an Intel system these three pages will be overwritten with the MLE page-tables by UBERXMHF `init` as described previously. The MLE header is written into the MLE at the beginning of the fourth page, and serves no purpose when the `secure-loader` executes on an AMD platform. This scheme enables the UBERXMHF `secure-loader` to meet both AMD and Intel DRT requirements with a single build process.

Because the UBERXMHF `secure-loader` can be loaded anywhere in memory depending on the system memory map, the UBERXMHF `secure-loader` needs to obtain its load address during runtime in order to set up required code, data, and stack segments. While AMD platforms provide the base address in the EAX register, not all Intel platforms provide this information.[6] UBERXMHF `secure-loader` therefore uses a cross-processor solution to read and align the instruction pointer register to discover the base address. More specifically it uses the sequence: `call 1f; 1: popl %eax; andl $0xffff0000,` `%eax` which returns the runtime base address of the `secure-loader` in the EAX register.

Early DMA Protection

The UBERXMHF `secure-loader` is loaded via a DRT operation which automatically records a cryptographic hash of the `secure-loader` in the platform TPM. The `secure-loader` in turn measures the UBERXMHF runtime (including the core and the uberapp) and extends this measurement into the platform TPM before transferring control to the runtime. While DRT protects the UBERXMHF `secure-loader` memory from the entire platform, the UBERXMHF runtime is still vulnerable to DMA attacks from possibly malicious platform peripherals; A malicious peripheral can overwrite the runtime memory after the runtime is

---

[5]In practice, we have observed that SS still points inside the SINIT code region. Still, it is prudent not to depend upon this behavior.

[6]If GETSEC[CAPABILITIES] indicates that ECX will contain the MLE base address pointer upon entry into the MLE, we can use ECX as the base address on Intel systems.

measured but before control is transferred to the runtime. To prevent such attacks, the UBERXMHF secure-loader employs what we term "early" DMA protection as described below.

On the Intel platforms, the UBERXMHF secure-loader employs the platform IOMMU hardware in order to set up DMA protection over the UBERXMHF runtime code before measuring the runtime. The IOMMU hardware includes a set of protected memory registers (PLMBASE_REG, PLMLIMIT_REG and PMEN_REG) which can be programmed to contain the base address and limit of physical memory and turn on DMA protection for the specified range. UBERXMHF secure-loader programs these registers to include the UBERXMHF secure-loader and the UBERXMHF runtime.

On AMD platforms, the UBERXMHF secure-loader employs the Device Exclusion Vector (DEV) to set up early DMA protection. The DEV is a bitmap structure with each bit corresponding to a physical memory page in the system. If a bit is 1, then DMA is disallowed, otherwise DMA is allowed for the corresponding memory page. However, since the UBERXMHF secure-loader and UBERXMHF runtime are loaded at the top of system memory below 4 GB, this presents an interesting problem: To be able to set DMA protections on the runtime we typically require an array of size > 64 KB. However, the size of the UBERXMHF secure-loader is limited to 64 KB in total (code and data). UBERXMHF secure-loader circumvents this problem using a protected 8K buffer (corresponding to a maximum 128 MB runtime size) within its memory image. UBERXMHF secure-loader then computes the DEV bitmap base address depending on the physical base address of the protected buffer and the physical base address of the memory region where the secure-loader was loaded. This aligns the 8K protected buffer to cover the secure-loader and runtime memory range up to a maximum of 128 MB. UBERXMHF secure-loader then sets the entire 8K buffer bits to 1's thereby DMA protecting the runtime. Note that we do not care about DMA protecting other parts of the DEV bitmap except for our protected buffer which is already DMA protected since the secure-loader was started using a DRT operation.

6 UBERXMHF Implementation on ARM Platforms

We now describe the UBERXMHF implementation on commodity ARM hardware virtualized platforms. The current UBERXMHF ARM implementation as of this writing supports the low-cost ubiquitous Raspberry PI 3. It can run unmodified Raspbian distribution with the Raspbian Linux kernel shipped with the Raspberry PI. In addition, UBERXMHF can run the unmodified Emlid real-time Linux kernel. The current implementation has a very modest, 24 MB memory footprint. We present a brief overview of the Raspberry PI platform before discussing the various architectural elements and how they are implemented on the Raspberry PI platform.

6.1   Raspberry PI Platform Overview

When the Raspberry PI is powered on, the ARM cores are in reset state and the GPU boots up. At this point the system memory (SDRAM) is disabled. The GPU starts executing the first-stage bootloader from ROM in the SoC. The first-stage bootloader reads the boot-partition of the boot-media (e.g., SD card, USB) and loads the second-stage bootloader (bootcode.bin) into the GPU L2 cache, and transfers control to it.

The boot-partition begins at a fixed address and is of fixed length regardless of the OS. bootcode.bin enables SDRAM, and loads and passes execution to the GPU firmware (start.elf). start.elf then initializes DMA, mailboxes and interrupt controller functionality required for GPU operation, sets up the bus MMU to allow ARM access to system memory, and boots up all the ARM cores in EL2 mode.

All the ARM cores except for the boot-strap ARM core are then placed within a mailbox wait-loop. start.elf then loads the OS kernel image (kernel.img) transfers control to it on the boot-strap ARM core. Lastly, kernel.img gets control, boots up, loads all the required OS drivers, and initializes the remaining ARM cores via a mailbox signal to establish a multi-core OS execution environment.

A more detailed security-oriented discussion of the Raspberry PI hardware platform along with all the hardware elements can be found in Vasudevan and Chaki (2018).

6.2   Rich-Guest Execution Model

6.2.1   Uberguest Memory Reporting

A native ARM OS during its bootup on the Raspberry PI has the option of using either the Device Tree Blob (DTB) or ATAGS in order to obtain the system memory map.[7] The DTB and ATAGS are essentially flat data structures that contain information about system memory and devices and various memory regions and their attributes (e.g., device MMIO, usable memory, and reserved). The DTB and ATAGS are set up by the GPU firmware prior to loading kernel.img.

However, with UBERXMHF loaded there must be a way to report a reduced memory map excluding the UBERXMHF memory regions to the OS. If not, the OS at some point during execution will end up accessing the UBERXMHF framework which would cause a fault since UBERXMHF memory is marked no-access within the second-stage page-tables (Sect. 6.4.1). UBERXMHF revises the DTB and

---

[7]Linux kernels adhere to this requirement. However, Windows IoT core uses an open-source UEFI bootloader which does not adhere to this requirement and uses values specified during build time. The UEFI bootloader source has to be modified to use the ATAGS/DTB instead.

the ATAGS structures adding entries to mark the UBERXMHF memory regions reserved. Thus a well-behaved OS will not attempt to access the UBERXMHF memory regions during the lifetime of its execution.[8]

6.2.2 Multi-Core Guest Boot-Up

On the Raspberry PI only one ARM core called the boot-strap core is started when the GPU firmware transfers control to kernel.img. The other (application) cores spin on the core mailbox waiting for a signal to awaken. At some point during the boot process of a native OS, the kernel will signal the mailbox which causes the other cores to awaken and start executing kernel code. UBERXMHF on boot-up initializes all the cores to EL2 mode and leaves all the application cores spinning on their mailbox and letting the boot-strap core start the OS in EL1 mode. When the OS signals the mailbox, the cores spinning in EL2 mode respond by grabbing the starting address (written to the mailbox) and transfers control to the OS in EL1 mode at the starting address.

6.3 μHV Core and Uberguest

The Raspberry PI boot-partition kernel.img (Sect. 6.1) is replaced by a unified UBERXMHF binary image consisting of: the UBERXMHF trampoline code; the original unmodified (uberguest) kernel.img; and the UBERXMHF μHV core and uberapp bundle. The UBERXMHF trampoline essentially transfers control to the UBERXMHF μHV core which in turn prepares the platform for uberguest and uberapp execution.

The UBERXMHF μHV core performs the following operations: (a) initializes μHV EL2 page-tables and the ARMv8 platform hardware virtualization support; (b) sets up memory, DMA, interrupt, and boot protections; and (c) transfers control to the uberguest kernel to start the OS boot process.

6.4 Uberguest Isolation

6.4.1 Uberguest Memory Isolation

UBERXMHF uses ARMv8 support for second-stage page-tables to implement uberguest memory isolation on ARM hardware platforms. The second-stage

---

[8]A malicious OS can still try to access the UBERXMHF memory regions, but will cause a fault in the second-stage page-tables; currently this causes UBERXMHF to ignore the access and resume the OS.

page-tables is a 3-level structure describing the guest physical address mappings to actual system addresses with additional protection bits (device, no-access, read–write, etc.). UBERXMHF framework regions (where the second-stage page-tables themselves reside) are marked no-access while other guest memory regions are marked read–write–execute. The VTCR register is then set to activate a 3-level page-table format with appropriate shareability and cacheability attributes (inner shareable and write-back, write-allocate caching). Finally, the VTTBR register is loaded with the base of the second-stage page-tables and second-stage page-table translation is enabled via the HCR register.

6.4.2 μHV Core Peripheral and Interrupt Partitioning

In the ARM ecosystem all system peripheral accesses happen via memory-mapped IO (MMIO). UBERXMHF by default maps all system peripherals with read–write protections except for the root interrupt controller, DMA controllers, and the MMC/SDHOST controller which are set up as described in Sects. 6.5.2, 6.7.1, and 6.8, respectively. UBERXMHF uses the hardware second-stage page-tables for such mappings. Note, other system peripherals can be set up on demand if required to be used exclusively by the UBERXMHF framework and uberapps (e.g., a watchdog uberapp and the hardware watchdog peripheral).

ARM uses FIQ signaling for fast interrupts and IRQ signaling for normal interrupts. The μHV core programs the HCR register to indicate no-trapping on IRQs. This allows uberguest to handle all peripheral interrupts without any intervention by UBERXMHF. UBERXMHF also sets the FIQ redirection bit in the HCR register for fast interrupt redirection to the μHV core. When this bit is set, hardware transfers control to a set location in EL2 mode on FIQ interrupts. The corresponding peripheral interrupt is then handled and cleared within the μHV core and/or the uberapp as required.

6.5   Uberapps and Uberapp Interactions

6.5.1   Synchronous Uberapp Interactions

ARMv8 hardware virtualization traps provide a hardware enforced mechanism for synchronous uberapp interactions. The HVC instruction is used to perform a hypercall and is used as a primary means for synchronous uberapp interactions from the uberguest. Other synchronous uberapp interactions happen via hardware assisted trap mechanisms including second-stage page-faults (as a result of protection violation in the second-stage page-tables) and designated instruction traps (e.g., execution of system instructions). Upon all such traps, the μHV core gets control, marshals required parameters and transfers control to the corresponding uberapp handlers.

6.5.2 Asynchronous Uberapp Interactions

The Raspberry PI Cortex-A53 ARM processor has support for per-core physical timers. The physical timers are banked across all the operating modes. The EL2 mode physical timer is controlled via a group of system registers which include the timer-value register (CNTHP_TVAL), compare value register (CNTHP_CVAL), and a control register (CNTHP_CTL). The timer-value is the physical timer and is incremented every clock cycle. The control register is programmed to trigger an interrupt if it matches the compare value register, UBERXMHF programs the root interrupt controller to generate a FIQ interrupt for interrupts received via the EL2 mode physical timer. The FIQ interrupt handler within the μHV core is responsible for invoking the corresponding uberapp timer handler for any periodic processing.

6.6 Attested Measurements

As described previously for x86 platforms (see Sect. 5.5), the UBERXMHF implementation on the ARM platform also includes the UBERXMHF secure-loader and UBERXMHF runtime as the two key components. Similar to the case of x86 platforms, during the uberapp build process, the UBERXMHF runtime components and the UBERXMHF secure-loader are built and the expected ("golden") hash itself is computed from the UBERXMHF secure-loader and runtime binaries using a utility such as sha1sum. This "golden" hash can be used to compare the result of a platform attestation to convince a local or remote verifier that UBERXMHF and the uberapp executed on the platform.

On ARM platforms UBERXMHF uses a static root-of-trust measurement to measure the values of the UBERXMHF runtime components. The measurement is carried out through a software TPM implementation called the micro-TPM.

The UBERXMHF micro TPM is based on the TrustVisor open-source x86 micro-TPM library implementation.[9,10] The micro-TPM implementation contains the library operations of PCR extend, read, seal, and unseal along with related private key storage and allows measuring and extending desired components and memory regions at runtime. The micro-TPM implementation currently uses ephemeral keys, but long-term storage can be achieved using the protected boot-partition (see Sect. 4) and/or the Raspberry PI NVRAM.

Note that uberapps can also interface with the micro-TPM via synchronous uberapp calls to implement uberapp specific attestation mechanism (e.g., approved code execution, encrypted filesystems, etc.)

---

[9]http://uberxmhf.org.

[10]While adding a physical TPM on the Raspberry PI is also an option, a software TPM has more advantages both in terms of cost, flexibility as well as performance (McCune et al., 2010).

6.7 Protections via Trap-Inspect-Forward

6.7.1 DMA Protection

The Raspberry PI contains a legacy DMA controller and a USB DMA controller on the SoC (Vasudevan and Chaki, 2018).

Legacy DMA Controller The legacy DMA controller contains 16 DMA channels and each channel is interfaced via a pair of registers: the control block address register and the status and enable register. The DMA control block (dmacb) structure consists of the source and destination DMA physical addresses along with the length of transfer and the address of the next control block structure. This way multiple control blocks can be linked in order to perform batch DMA operations. The legacy DMA controller is MMIO mapped in the second-stage page-tables with a no-access protection. This allows trapping on both reads and writes to channel pair registers.

UBERXMHF uses DMA control block shadowing in order to protect framework memory from (malicious) DMA transactions. On write to the dmacb address register, we iterate through the control block list supplied by the OS and copy it over to a μHV core control block area. During this copy we also ensure that the control block source and destination do not include any UBERXMHF memory regions. We then set the dmacb address register to the address of the shadow control block. Subsequent write to the DMA enable register by the OS will then use the shadow control block for DMA transfers. Similarly, reads to the control block address will return the original control block address as expected by the OS. This shadowing mechanism is both efficient and effective in terms of preventing any form of DMA attacks including DMA gadgets (Rushanan and Checkoway, 2015).

USB DMA Controller The Raspberry PI also consists of a USB DMA controller which is part of the USB OTG host controller. The usbdmac consists of various registers which form a DMA descriptor. One such address is the host address which is used to transfer USB data into or out of the system. The usbdmac is mapped as MMIO in the second-stage page-table with read-only protection. This allows us to pass through descriptor reads any trap only on writes. On write trapping via second-stage page-faults we check to ensure that the value written to the host address field is part of the uberguest memory region. If not, the write is denied.

6.7.2 Interrupt Protection

The Raspberry PI root interrupt controller (RIC) is employed for interrupt partitioning for peripherals that are reserved exclusively for the μHV core and/or uberapps. The EL2 timer is one such example which is used by the μHV core for periodic uberapp processing. The RIC contains an interrupt enable and interrupt type field for physical timers as well as other system peripherals.

UBERXMHF maps the RIC as MMIO and with read-only protections in the second-stage page-tables. This allows us to intercept on writes to the RIC registers while allowing reads to pass through. The current implementation ignores any writes to the interrupt enable and interrupt type fields for the EL2 timer peripheral. This ensures that EL2 timer interrupts for periodic uberapp processing are always fired.

6.8 Secure Boot

The UBERXMHF secure boot implementation on Raspberry PI supports any SD card that is complaint to the SDIO v3 standard. This is the same requirement imposed by the Raspberry PI itself. As per the SDIO specification, before any operation (read or write) is performed on the card, the MMC/SDHOST controller ARG register is set to the actual sector address for performing the operation and the BLKCOUNT register is set to the number of blocks that needs to be taken into account. This is then followed by a write to the SDCMD register which specifies if a read (17/18) or write (24/25) operation is to be performed. For example, to write a sector at address 0 on the SD card the ARG register is set to 0, BLKCOUNT register is set to 1, and the SDCMD register is set to 24.

UBERXMHF maps the SD HOST controller register space as MMIO and read-only in the second-stage page-tables. This allows us to only trap on writes to the register space allowing reads to pass through thereby preventing unnecessary traps due to any status condition reads via the register address space. Upon a write to the SDCMD register for a write command, UBERXMHF checks the ARG and the BLKCOUNT register to ensure that they do not fall within the boot-partition sector range. This is a fixed range for the Raspberry PI regardless of the running OS (see Sect. 6.1). If UBERXMHF detects writes that fall within the boot-partition sector range, it ignores the write and sets the status register to indicate an error, else the write command is allowed to go through.

7 Evaluation

We present the trusted computing base (TCB) size of UBERXMHF's current implementation and follow up with a discussion on the security analysis of the UBERXMHF architecture in the context of our attacker model and system assumptions (Sect. 2.4). Interested readers can refer to Vasudevan et al. (2013); Vasudevan and Chaki (2018) for a more in-depth framework performance evaluation.

7.1 Trusted Computing Base (TCB)

Like all security systems, UBERXMHF must assume the correctness and security of its components. One way to make this assumption more likely to hold is to keep things modular and reduce the amount of code and complexity that must be trusted. This in turn reduces the opportunity for bugs. UBERXMHF's TCB comprises of runtime libraries, μHV core, and uberapps. The runtime libraries currently include a tiny C, crypto and micro-TPM library. The μHV core comprises of base platform code, uberguest and uberapps support, secure boot, memory, DMA and interrupt protection mechanisms. Combining everything, UBERXMHF's SLoC is around 14000 SLoC including every function in all supporting libraries.

UBERXMHF's SLoC and modular implementation is well within range for state-of-the-art system software verification approaches (Vasudevan et al., 2016; Gu et al., 2015; Vasudevan et al., 2013) to be readily applied to the code base for higher assurance. UBERXMHF's SLoC is also an order of magnitude smaller than other traditional hypervisors on commodity x86 and ARM platforms (e.g., Xen: approx. 150K SLoC, Xvisor (Patel et al., 2015): approx. 265K SLoC; KVM (Dall et al., 2016) within Linux Kernel: in millions of SLoC).

7.2   UBERXMHF *Security Analysis*

We now present a security analysis of the UBERXMHF architecture in the context of our attacker model and system assumptions (Sect. 2.4).

UBERXMHF's secure boot mechanism (Sect. 3.8) ensures that a valid UBERXMHF image will always be loaded during boot-up or that a valid loaded image can be attested to. The former is enforced by preventing writes to the boot-partition of UBERXMHF. With the UBERXMHF installation ensuring a legitimate copy of the boot-partition to begin with (see Sect. 4), this ensures a valid UBERXMHF image will always be loaded during boot-up. UBERXMHF's use of the TPM ensures that a remote platform can verify the integrity of the loaded UBERXMHF image.

UBERXMHF's use of hardware second-stage page-tables ensures that code executing within the uberguest cannot directly address the μHV core or uberapps, thus protecting their secrecy and integrity. Thus, even though a uberguest can be exploited via software or network vulnerabilities, such exploits cannot compromise the μHV core or uberapps directly.

UBERXMHF's DMA protection mechanism ensures that malicious peripherals (e.g., USB, SPI, or I2C peripherals) can only access uberguest memory regions, and prevents advanced DMA controller-based attacks such as DMA gadgets (Rushanan and Checkoway, 2015).

Finally, UBERXMHF's support for periodic uberapps and interrupt partitioning prevents malware in the uberguest from carrying out a denial of service (DoS) attack on UBERXMHF. Note that malware in the uberguest can mount a DoS attack on synchronous uberapps by compromising the uberguest application that is bound to the uberapp. However, such DoS attacks can be detected (e.g., by employing a watchdog uberapp).

8 Summary

Taking stock of the current crop of commodity (x86 and ARM) computing platforms, our overarching goal is to realize practical performant security with a low TCB, and without sacrificing commodity compatibility.

The uber eXtensible Micro-Hypervisor Framework (UBERXMHF) strives to be a comprehensible and flexible platform for building micro-hypervisor assisted security-sensitive applications ("uberapps"). By providing in a modular way not only most of the infrastructure "grunge" needed by an application looking to protect sensitive information, but also supporting libraries, UBERXMHF's goal is to lower the barrier to develop new and exciting uberapps with a low TCB while being compatible with unmodified legacy operating systems and applications. Chapter "Micro-Hypervisor Applications" describes several such applications that have been developed.

Work is underway to build upon the low-TCB and low complexity nature of UBERXMHF to perform formal verification for higher assurance. Given UBERXMHF's features and performance characteristics, we anticipate that it will continue to significantly enhance security-oriented micro-hypervisor research and development.

9 Availability

Active, open-source development of the uber eXtensible Micro-Hypervisor Framework continues at: https://uberxmhf.org

References

Advanced Micro Devices (2005) AMD64 architecture programmer's manual: volume 2: system programming. AMD, Publication no. 24594 rev. 3.11

ARM Limited (2010) Virtualization extensions architecture specification. http://infocenter.arm. com

Ben-Yehuda M, Day MD, Dubitzky Z, Factor M, Har'El N, Gordon A, Liguori A, Wasserman O, Yassour BA (2010) The turtles project: design and implementation of nested virtualization. In: Proceedings of OSDI 2010

Boileau A (2006) Hit by a bus: physical access attacks with firewire. Ruxcon

Chen X, Garfinkel T, Lewis EC, Subrahmanyam P, Waldspurger CA, Boneh D, Dwoskin J, Ports DRK (2008) Overshadow: a virtualization-based approach to retrofitting protection in commodity operating systems. In: Proceedings of ASPLOS

Dall C, Li SW, Lim JT, Nieh J, Koloventzos G (2016) Arm virtualization: performance and architectural implications. SIGARCH Comput Archit News 44(3):304–316. http://doi.acm.org/10.1145/3007787.3001169

Dinaburg A, Royal P, Sharif M, Lee W (2008) Ether: malware analysis via hardware virtualization extensions. In: Proceedings of ACM CCS 2008

Elhage N (2011) Virtunoid: breaking out of KVM. Defcon

Fattori A, Paleari R, Martignoni L, Monga M (2010) Dynamic and transparent analysis of commodity production systems. In: Proceedings of IEEE/ACM ASE 2010

Garfinkel T, Pfaff B, Chow J, Rosenblum M, Boneh D (2003) Terra: a virtual machine-based platform for trusted computing. In: ACM SOSP

Gordon A, Ben-Yehuda M, Amit N, HarÉl N, Landau A, Schuster A (2012) ELI: bare-metal performance for I/O virtualization. In: Architectural support for programming languages and operating systems (ASPLOS)

Gu R, Koenig J, Ramananandro T, Shao Z, Wu XN, Weng SC, Zhang H, Guo Y (2015) Deep specifications and certified abstraction layers. In: Proceedings of POPL

Intel Corporation (2005) IA-32 Intel architecture software developer's manual. Intel Publication nos. 253665–253668

Intel Corporation (2006) Trusted execution technology–preliminary architecture specification and enabling considerations. Document number 31516803

Karger P, Safford D (2008) I/O for virtual machine monitors: security and performance issues. IEEE Secur Priv 6(5). https://doi.org/10.1109/MSP.2008.119

Litty L, Lagar-Cavilla HA, Lie D (2008) Hypervisor support for identifying covertly executing binaries. In: Proceedings of USENIX security symposium

McCune JM, Li Y, Qu N, Zhou Z, Datta A, Gligor V, Perrig A (2010) TrustVisor: efficient TCB reduction and attestation. In: Proceedings of IEEE S&P

Patel A, Daftedar M, Shalan M, El-Kharashi MW (2015) Embedded hypervisor Xvisor: a comparative analysis. In: Proceedings of the 23rd Euromicro international conference on parallel, distributed, and network-based processing, pp 682–691. https://doi.org/10.1109/PDP.2015.108

Quist D, Liebrock L, Neil J (2011) Improving antivirus accuracy with hypervisor assisted analysis. J Comput Virol 7(2):121–131

Rushanan M, Checkoway S (2015) Run-DMA. In: Proceedings of USENIX workshop on offensive technology (WOOT)

Seshadri A, Luk M, Qu N, Perrig A (2007) SecVisor: a tiny hypervisor to provide lifetime kernel code integrity for commodity OSes. In: Proceedings of SOSP

Sharif MI, Lee W, Cui W, Lanzi A (2009) Secure in-VM monitoring using hardware virtualization. In: Proceedings of ACM CCS

Singaravelu L, Pu C, Haertig H, Helmuth C (2006) Reducing TCB complexity for security-sensitive applications: three case studies. In: Proceedings of EuroSys

Ta-Min R, Litty L, Lie D (2006) Splitting interfaces: making trust between applications and operating systems configurable. In: Proceedings of SOSP

Trusted Computing Group (2005) PC client specific TPM interface specification (TIS). Version 1.2, Revision 1.00

Trusted Computing Group (2007) Trusted platform module main specification. Version 1.2, Revision 103

Vasudevan A, Chaki S (2018) Have your PI and eat it too: practical security on a low-cost ubiquitous computing platform. In: 2018 IEEE European symposium on security and privacy, EuroS&P 2018, London, United Kingdom, April 24–26, 2018, pp 183–198. https://doi.org/10.1109/EuroSP.2018.00021

Vasudevan A, Qu N, Perrig A (2011) XTRec: secure real-time execution trace recording on commodity platforms. In: Proceedings of IEEE HICSS

Vasudevan A, Parno B, Qu N, Gligor VD, Perrig A (2012) Lockdown: towards a safe and practical architecture for security applications on commodity platforms. In: Proceedings of TRUST

Vasudevan A, Chaki S, Jia L, McCune J, Newsome J, Datta A (2013) Design, implementation and verification of an extensible and modular hypervisor framework. In: Proceedings of 2013 IEEE symposium on security and privacy

Vasudevan A, Chaki S, Maniatis P, Jia L, Datta A (2016) überSpark: enforcing verifiable object abstractions for automated compositional security analysis of a hypervisor. In: 25th USENIX security symposium (USENIX security 16), USENIX Association, Austin, TX, pp 87–104. https://www.usenix.org/conference/usenixsecurity16/technical-sessions/presentation/vasudevan

Wang Z, Jiang X (2010) HyperSafe: a lightweight approach to provide lifetime hypervisor control-flow integrity. In: Proceedings of IEEE S&P

Wang Z, Wu C, Grace M, Jiang X (2012) Isolating commodity hosted hypervisors with HyperLock. In: Proceedings of EuroSys 2012

Xen (2011a) Xen PCI passthrough. http://wiki.xensource.com/xenwiki/XenPCIpassthrough

Xen (2011b) Xen VGA passthrough. http://wiki.xensource.com/xenwiki/XenVGAPassthrough

Xen (2011c) Xen VTd HowTo. http://wiki.xensource.com/xenwiki/VTdHowTo

Xiong X, Tian D, Liu P (2011) Practical protection of kernel integrity for commodity OS from untrusted extensions. In: Proceedings of NDSS 2011

Zhang F, Chen J, Chen H, Zang B (2011) CloudVisor: retrofitting protection of virtual machines in multi-tenant cloud with nested virtualization. In: Proceedings of SOSP

Micro-Hypervisor Applications

Abstract This chapter showcases several micro-hypervisor-based applications ("uberapps") that employ uberXMHF. These uberapps span a wide spectrum of security applications including application compartmentalization and sandboxing, attestation, approved code execution, key management, tracing, verifiable resource accounting, trusted-path, and on-demand I/O isolation. They showcase the efficacy and versatility of a micro-hypervisor-based system security architecture.

1 Introduction

Over the past-decade several micro-hypervisor applications have emerged and demonstrated the utility for realizing practical security properties with a low trusted computing base on commodity platforms. In this chapter we enumerate a representative collection of uberapps that extend the base micro-hypervisor system architecture in unique ways to implement a variety of practical security properties on today's commodity platforms. Below are the application domains we discuss in this chapter:

- Red/Green Compartmentalization
- Attestation
- Approved Execution
- Key Management
- Resource Accounting
- Sandboxing
- Execution Tracing
- Trusted Path
- On-demand I/O Isolation

We limit the scope of our discussion in each of the application domains to high-level architectural details. Interested readers can follow the included pointers to corresponding seminal research for a more in-depth and exhaustive discussion.

A. Vasudevan, *Practical Security Properties on Commodity Computing Platforms*,
SpringerBriefs in Computer Science, https://doi.org/10.1007/978-3-030-25049-2_4

2   Red-Green Compartmentalization

Consumers currently use their general-purpose computers to perform many sensitive tasks; they pay bills, fill out tax forms, check account balances, trade stocks, and access medical data. Unfortunately, increasingly sophisticated and ubiquitous attacks undermine the security of these activities. Red/green systems (Lampson, 2009; Peinado et al., 2004) have been proposed as a mechanism for improving user security without abandoning the generality that has made computers so successful. They are based on the observation that users perform security-sensitive transactions infrequently, and hence enhanced security protections need only be provided on demand for a limited set of activities. Thus, with a red/green system, the user spends most of her time in a general-purpose, untrusted (or *red*) environment which retains the full generality of her normal computer; i.e., she can install arbitrary applications that run with good performance. When the user wishes to perform a security-sensitive transaction, she switches to a trusted (or *green*) environment that includes stringent protections, managed code, network and services at the cost of some performance degradation.

Lockdown (Vasudevan et al., 2012) investigates a new point in the design space of red/green systems, to provide the user with a highly protected, yet also highly constrained trusted ("green") environment for performing security-sensitive transactions, as well as a high-performance, general-purpose environment for all other (non-security-sensitive or "red") applications.

In particular, Lockdown leverages the micro-hypervisor system architecture to partition system resources across time, so that only one environment (trusted or untrusted) runs at a time. When switching between the two environments, Lockdown resets the state of the system (including devices) and leverages existing support for platform power-management to save and restore device state. This approach makes Lockdown device agnostic, removes considerable complexity from the hypervisor, and yet maintains binary compatibility with existing free and commercial operating systems (e.g., Windows and Linux run unmodified). It also allows the untrusted environment to have unfettered access to devices, resulting in near native performance for most applications, although a small performance degradation is necessary to protect Lockdown from the untrusted environment.

In the trusted environment, Lockdown employs more expensive mechanisms to keep the environment pristine. For example, Lockdown only permits known, trusted code to execute. Since this trusted code may still contain bugs, Lockdown ensures that trusted applications can only communicate with trusted sites. This prevents malicious sites from corrupting the applications, and ensures that even if a trusted application is corrupted, it can only leak data to sites the user already trusts with her data.

In addition, Lockdown provides a user interface for red/green systems that is independent of the platform. A small, external USB device communicates the state of the system (i.e., trusted or untrusted) to the user. The security display is beyond the control of an adversary and cannot be spoofed or manipulated. Its simple interface (providing essentially one bit of input and one bit of output) makes it easy to understand and use, and overcomes the challenges in user-based attestation (McCune et al., 2007) to create a trusted communication channel between the user and the red/green system.

3 Efficient Attestation

Current commodity operating systems and the majority of applications lack assurance that the secrecy and integrity of security-sensitive code and data are protected. The size and complexity of current commodity operating systems and applications suggest that we will not achieve the level of assurance necessary to run security-sensitive code and data on these platforms in the near future. Yet, commodity platforms offer unmatched incentives for both casual users and developers, and hence will remain a dominant presence in the marketplace.

TrustVisor (McCune et al., 2010) protects small security-sensitive code blocks within a potentially malicious environment and yet achieves high performance for legacy applications. More specifically, TrustVisor provides data secrecy and integrity, as well as execution integrity for security-sensitive portions of an application, executing the code in isolation from the OS, untrusted application code, and system devices. Execution integrity is the property that a piece of code actually executes with prescribed inputs produces desired outputs. Finally, TrustVisor also enables external entities to receive attestations that describe the execution of security-sensitive code and optionally its parameters to a remote party.

To accomplish these goals, TrustVisor leverages a micro-hypervisor-based system architecture that is designed to provide a measured, isolated execution environment for security-sensitive code modules without trusting the OS or the application that invokes the code module. This environment is initialized via a process similar to dynamic root of trust (DRTM) (Advanced Micro Devices, 2007; Intel Corporation, 2008), called the TrustVisor Root of Trust for Measurement or TRTM. TRTM interacts with a software-based, *micro-TPM* (uTPM) that is part of TrustVisor and executes at high speed on the platform's primary CPU.

TrustVisor employs a two-level approach to integrity measurement. This mechanism enables attestation of the code and execution integrity properties of security-sensitive code blocks, and also enables these code blocks to seal data by encrypting it such that decryption is only possible if the right set of integrity measurements are present. The first-level mechanism employed is a system's physical TPM chip, and the second level is implemented in software via the *micro-TPM* that is part of TrustVisor. The uTPM is restricted to providing only basic randomness, measurement, attestation, and data sealing facilities. Additional trusted computing features can be leveraged by directly interacting with the hardware TPM.

4   Approved Execution

Computing platforms are steadily increasing in complexity, incorporating an ever-growing range of hardware and supporting an ever-growing range of applications. Consequently, the complexity of OS kernels has been steadily increasing. The increased complexity of OS kernels also increases the number of security vulnerabilities. The effect of these vulnerabilities is compounded by the fact that, despite many efforts to make kernels modular, most kernels in common use today are monolithic in their design. A compromise of any part of a monolithic kernel could compromise the entire kernel. Since the kernel occupies a privileged position in the software stack of a computer system, compromising it gives the attacker complete control of the system. In view of the importance of the security of the kernel to the security of a system, securing existing kernels is of critical importance.

SecVisor (Seshadri et al., 2007) provides a lifetime guarantee of the integrity of the code executing with kernel privilege. SecVisor leverages a micro-hypervisor-based architecture to avoid mandating large-scale design changes. SecVisor prevents an attacker from either modifying existing code in a kernel or from executing injected code with kernel privilege, over the lifetime of the system. Furthermore, SecVisor can achieve this guarantee even in the presence of an attacker who controls everything on the system except for the CPU, memory controller, and system memory chips. SecVisor ensures that only code approved by the user can execute with kernel privilege. Users can supply their desired approval policy and SecVisor checks all code loaded into the kernel against the users' approval policy. It further ensures that the approved code currently in memory cannot be modified by the attacker.

SecVisor prevents numerous attacks against current kernels. For example, there are at least three ways in which an attacker can inject code into a kernel. First, the attacker can misuse the modularization support that is part of many current kernels. Modularization support allows privileged users to add code to the running kernel. An attacker can employ a privilege escalation attack to load a module into the kernel. Second, the attacker can locally or remotely exploit software vulnerabilities in the kernel code. For example, the attacker can inject code by overflowing a vulnerable kernel buffer. Third, DMA-capable peripheral devices can corrupt kernel memory via DMA writes. A sample attack that uses FireWire peripherals was demonstrated by Becher et al. (2005).

SecVisor uses micro-hypervisor second-stage hardware memory protections to ensure kernel code integrity. This allows SecVisor to set hardware protections over kernel memory, which are independent of any protections set by the kernel. SecVisor also uses the IO Memory Management Unit (IOMMU) to protect approved code from Direct Memory Access (DMA) writes. Finally, SecVisor virtualizes the CPU's Memory Management Unit (MMU) and the IOMMU. This ensures that SecVisor can intercept and check all modifications to MMU and IOMMU state that can violate the approved code execution protections.

5 Key Management

As consumers and corporations are increasingly concerned about security, deployments of cryptographic systems and protocols have grown from securing online banking and ecommerce to web email, search, social networking, and sensitive data protection. However, the security guarantees diminish with inadequate key management practices, as exemplified by numerous real-world incidents (Matrosov et al., 2019; Vasco , 2011).

There are at least two significant challenges that come into play when designing any secure key management system (KMS).

- **Fine-grained Key Usage Control.** A comprehensive life-cycle KMS should enforce fine-grained key usage control (i.e., whether an application operated by a user has the permission to access a specific cryptographic key). This problem is exacerbated with the current trend of Bring Your Own Device (BYOD), which allows client devices (e.g., tablets and laptops) to increasingly host both personal and security-sensitive corporate applications and data.
- **Secure System Administration.** A trustworthy KMS should allow benign administrators to securely manage the system and defend against attacks from malicious insiders. It must guarantee the authenticity of the communication between the administrators and the KMS. Otherwise, an adversary can cause unintended key management operations by stealing administrator login credentials, modifying or spoofing the administrator command input or the KMS output (e.g., operation result, system status).

KISS (short for Key it Simple and Secure) (Zhou et al., 2013) is a comprehensive, trustworthy, user-verifiable, and cost-effective enterprise key management architecture. KISS leverages a micro-hypervisor-based system architecture to protect the key management software and cryptographic keys from the large untrusted OS, applications, and peripheral devices. The administrators securely bootstrap the KISS system using the simple administrator devices and lightweight protocols, regardless of malware attacks and insider attacks from malicious administrators. These mechanisms together significantly reduce and simplify the KISS TCB, enabling higher security assurance.

KISS supports fine-grained key usage control based on users, applications, and configurable access control policies. To do this, KISS isolates authorized corporate applications from the untrusted OS and measures the code identities (cryptographic hash) of the protected applications. KISS also directly accepts user authentication by isolating user-interface devices and authentication relevant devices from the OS. Moreover, KISS enables secure system administration, leveraging a simple external device with minimal software/hardware settings. The KISS administrators execute thin terminal software on commodity machines. The thin terminal accepts administrator input via trusted paths, remotely transfers the input to and receives system output from the KISS system. The administrators use the external devices to verify the execution of the thin terminal and trusted paths and guarantee the authenticity of the input/output.

KISS showcases how micro-hypervisor-based system architecture combined with commodity hardware trusted computing primitives achieves tangible benefits when used to design trustworthy KMS.

6 Verifiable Resource Accounting

The computing-as-a-service model—enterprises and businesses outsourcing their applications and services to cloud-based deployments—is mainstay today. Surveys indicate that 61% of IT executives and CIOs rated the "pay only for what you use" as a very important perceived benefit of the cloud model and more than 80% of respondents rated competitive pricing and performance assurances/Service-Level Agreements (SLAs) as important benefits (IDC, 2013).

Anecdotal evidence suggests that customers perceive a disconnect between their workloads and charges (Mihoob et al., 2010; Cohen, 2019; Bil, 2009; Sha, 2011). At the same time, providers suffer too as they are unable to accurately justify resource costs. For example, providers today do not account for memory bandwidth, internal network resources, power/cooling costs, or I/O stress (Iyer et al., 2009; Wachs et al., 2011; Mogul, 2005). This accounting inaccuracy and uncertainty creates economic inefficiency, as providers lose revenue from undercharging or customers lose confidence from overcharging. While trust in cloud providers may be a viable model for some, others may prefer "trust but verify" given providers' incentive to overcharge. Such guaranteed resource accounting is especially important to counter demonstrated attacks on cloud accounting (Somorovsky et al., 2011; Zhou et al., 2011; Liu and Ding, 2010).

Alibi (Chen et al., 2013) addresses the challenge to achieve verifiable resource accounting with *low overhead* and *minimal changes* to existing deployment models. Alibi proposes a system architecture towards a vision for *verifiable resource accounting*. Alibi places a minimal, trusted reference monitor underneath the service provider's software platform; the monitor observes resource allocation to customers' guest virtual machines and reports those observations to customers, for verifiable reconciliation. To this end, Alibi benefits from a micro-hypervisor-based system architecture coupled with recent advances in *nested virtualization*. Specifically, Alibi's architecture encompasses a thin lightweight micro-hypervisor atop which today's legacy hypervisors and guest operating systems can run with minor or no modification. Thus, this approach lends itself to an immediately deployable alternative for current provider and customer side infrastructures.

Alibi further identifies and extends appropriate resource allocation "chokepoints" using a combination of hardware nested virtualization support and memory protections to provide the necessary hooks, while guaranteeing that customer jobs run untampered while at the same time efficiently and verifiably tracking guests' memory use and CPU-cycle consumption. Alibi demonstrates that: (1) verifiable accounting is possible and efficient in the existing cloud-computing usage model; (2) nested virtualization coupled with a micro-hypervisor-based system security architecture is an effective mechanism to provide trustworthy resource accounting; and (3) a number of documented accounting attacks can be thus thwarted.

7 Application Sandboxing

Platform-as-a-Service (PaaS) is one of the most widely commercialized forms of cloud computing. On PaaS cloud computing, it is critical to protect the cloud platform from the large number of untrusted applications sent by customers. Thus, a virtualized infrastructure (e.g., Xen (Barham et al., 2003)) and sandbox (e.g., Java sandbox (Gong, 2018)) are typically deployed to isolate customer's applications and protect the guest OS. However, security on PaaS is not only a concern for cloud providers but also a concern for cloud customers. The security-sensitive portions of the application logic are completely exposed to malicious code on the OS.

MiniBox (Li et al., 2014) proposes a security model for PaaS cloud computing by introducing a "two-way" sandboxing mechanism. The two-way sandbox not only protects a benign OS from a misbehaving application (OS protection) but also protects an application from a malicious OS (application protection).

MiniBox provides a two-way sandbox for x86 native applications. Leveraging a micro-hypervisor-based system architecture and memory isolation mechanism and a mature one-way sandbox such as Google Native Client (NaCl) (Yee et al., 2009), MiniBox offers efficient two-way protection. MiniBox splits the NaCl sandbox into OS protection modules (software modules performing OS protection) and service runtime (software modules supporting application execution), runs the service runtime and the application in an isolated memory space, and exposes a minimized and secure communication interface between the OS protection modules and the application.

MiniBox also splits the system call interface available to the isolated application as sensitive calls (the calls that may cause Iago attacks (Checkoway and Shacham, 2013)) and non-sensitive calls (the calls that cannot cause Iago attacks), and protects the application against Iago attacks by handling sensitive calls inside the service runtime in the isolated memory space. MiniBox also provides secure file I/O for the application. Using a special toolchain, application developers can concentrate on application development with small porting effort.

MiniBox demonstrates it is possible to leverage a micro-hypervisor- based system architecture to provide an efficient, minimized, and secure communication interface between OS protection modules and the application to protect against each other.

8 Trusted Path

A Trusted Path (TP) is a protected channel that assures the secrecy and authenticity of data transfers between a user's input/output (I/O) devices and a program trusted by that user. Without a trusted path, an adversary could surreptitiously obtain sensitive user-input data by recording key strokes, modify user commands to corrupt application-program operation, and display unauthentic program output to an unsuspecting user to trigger incorrect user action. This is particularly true for systems where an operator would be unable to determine the true state of a remote device and to control it in the presence of a malware-compromised commodity OS (Falliere et al., 2011; Meserve, 2007; Shachtman, 2011).

Designing and implementing a trusted path on any commodity computer system is met with a number of overarching challenges:

- **MMIO Mappings:** Address-space isolation alone is insufficient to remove device drivers from each-others' TCBs, because substantial shared device configuration state exists on commodity computers. A compromised driver in one domain can manipulate that state to compromise the secrecy and authenticity of communication between drivers in other domains and their corresponding devices. For example, a compromised driver can intentionally configure the memory-mapped I/O (MMIO) region of a device to overlap the MMIO region of another device. Such a manipulated device may then intercept MMIO access to the legitimate trusted-path device endpoint
- **Interrupt Spoofing:** Another significant challenge not met by address-space isolation is interrupt spoofing. Software-configurable interrupts (e.g., Message Signaled Interrupts (MSI) and Inter-processor Interrupts (IPI)) share the same interrupt vector space with hardware interrupts. By modifying the MSI registers of a device, a compromised driver may spoof the MSI interrupts of the device endpoint.
- **Verifiable Isolation:** Finally, another challenge is to provide trusted-path mechanisms with verifiable isolation properties on commodity platforms without resorting to external devices that protect and manage cryptographic secrets.

Zhou et al. (2012) address the aforementioned challenges by proposing a trusted-path design and implementation that isolates the trusted path from the untrusted OS, applications, and devices. The architecture comprises four components: a program endpoint (PE), a device endpoint(s) (DE), the communication-path, and a micro-hypervisor (uHV).

By leveraging a micro-hypervisor-based system security architecture (that directly runs on commodity hardware and supports a single guest OS), in lieu of a full-features hypervisor (e.g., VMware Workstation, Xen (Barham et al., 2003)), all the devices outside the trusted-path are directly visible to the OS which can operate on those devices without the involvement of the micro-hypervisor. For example, a regular untrusted application can access the devices outside the trusted-path via ordinary OS support. The uHV provides the necessary mechanisms to ensure isolation between program endpoints, device endpoints, and communication paths for trusted paths. In particular, the uHV isolates trusted-path device state from the "shared device-configuration state" on the commodity platform. The program endpoint PE of a trusted path includes the device drivers for DEs that are associated with that trusted path.

The trusted-path architecture proposed by Zhou et al. (2012) is general in that it allows arbitrary program endpoints running on arbitrary OSes to be isolated from their underlying OS and to establish a trusted path with arbitrary unmodified devices. It is trustworthy in that the TCB is very small—owing to the micro-hypervisor-based design—and simple enough to put it within the reach of formal verification. It is human-verifiable in that a human using the machine can verify that the desired trusted path is in effect (e.g., that the keyboard is acting as a secure channel to a banking program on that machine).

9 On-Demand I/O Isolation

Wimpy (Zhou et al., 2015) leverages a micro-hypervisor-based system architecture enabling secure composition with a large software system (e.g., untrusted OS) to provide on-demand isolated I/O services to application-level isolated security components. Wimpy is characterized by four system attributes: (a) generality: able to isolate any I/O software and support any peripheral I/O devices; (b) simplicity: has a small and simple code base to facilitate formal reasoning of its security properties; (c) commodity: compatible with commodity operating systems without requiring their restructuring or redesign; and (d) on demand: support on-demand I/O operation rather than be restricted to static device allocation.

In the on-demand I/O isolation model employed by Wimpy, an untrusted OS usually manages all commodity hardware resources and devices on the platform. However, when a security-sensitive application, demands exclusive use of a device, the I/O isolation system takes control of necessary hardware communication resources from the untrusted commodity OS, verifies the OS configurations, and allocates the configurations to the isolated security-sensitive application. When the application is done with a channel, the system returns all resources to the untrusted OS.

To provide on-demand isolated I/O channels on commodity systems with a small and simple code base, the Wimpy architecture builds on top of the micro-hypervisor system architecture (uHV) and by adding a small I/O kernel. The underlying uHV is a trustworthy component added supporting an existing untrusted commodity OS. The uHV provides a typical isolated execution environment for security-sensitive applications to defend against the untrusted OS and other untrusted applications. The uHV controls only the few hardware resources needed for code isolation, whereas the untrusted OS controls the remaining chipset hardware and peripheral devices.

The I/O kernel is an add-on, trustworthy component, which is isolated from an untrusted OS by uHV. It executes at the OS's privilege level, isolates itself from security-sensitive applications via traditional ring protection, dynamically controls the hardware resources necessary to establish isolated I/O channels between security-sensitive apps and I/O devices, and prevents the untrusted OS from interfering with these channels and vice versa. The security-sensitive apps use modified, unprivileged device drivers to communicate with the isolated I/O devices under the I/O kernel mediation.[1]

10 Execution Tracing

As the Internet expands to include billions of heterogeneous systems and devices, there is a growing need to develop a usable trust infrastructure which would allow interacting systems to better manage security risks. These risks could be mitigated by the availability of information establishing the relative trustworthiness of the systems involved during runtime. Such information (or its absence) could be used to select an appropriate threat posture as interaction is initiated or requested. Currently, one approach for trust evaluation of other systems is to use trusted computing-based attestation mechanisms, to validate the software integrity of the loaded software. The next frontier is to also achieve attestation for execution properties, such as control-flow properties. This increase in attestation granularity would help catch dynamic vulnerabilities that are invisible to standard software attestation.

XTRec (Vasudevan et al., 2011) is an offline instruction-level execution tracing system that runs on commodity platforms with x86-class CPUs and produces a secure instruction-level execution trace in real-time. XTRec leverages a micro-hypervisor-based system architecture and uses commodity hardware virtualization to provide robustness against subversion and maintain the integrity of the execution trace. Furthermore, XTRec does not entail any modifications to the host OS or applications and does not require ad hoc platform hardware. The instruction-level traces produced enable reconstruction of all instructions in the *exact* order they were executed. The design of XTRec collects execution traces of a host system during runtime and stores the traces on a remote system where trace processing is performed offline.

XTRec takes advantage of the branch trace messaging (BTM) feature found on all x86-class processors (Kurts et al., 2003).[2] BTMs are issued by the CPU on every taken conditional and unconditional branch instruction, and contain the memory address of the branch target. The BTMs are then superimposed on dynamically captured code pages to obtain a complete instruction-level execution

---

[1]Note that uHV and the I/O kernel *do not* form a reference monitor for the commodity OS because they do not mediate references to all OS devices.

[2]ARM processors have a similar feature known as Embedded Trace Macrocells.

trace. The micro-hypervisor-based design guarantees that XTRec and the recording mechanisms are isolated from and independent of the monitored program and OS. In the offline version, the collected traces are transmitted to a separate log store via a dedicated network connection.

Willems et al. (2012) employ a modification of XTrec to demonstrate the effectiveness and applicability of a micro-hypervisor-based system architecture coupled with localized processor branch trace messaging towards analyzing malicious PDF documents in real-time. In an empirical evaluation, they demonstrate that the branch tracing results can be used to automatically cluster similar vulnerabilities which are exploited within the analyzed documents (Willems et al., 2012). Most notably, such a framework can also deal with advanced exploits that use concepts like structured exception handler (SEH) for control flow diversion and even return-oriented programming.

References

Advanced Micro Devices (2007) AMD64 architecture programmer's manual. System programming, vol 2. AMD Publication no. 24593 rev. 3.14

Barham P, Dragovic B, Fraser K, Hand S, Harris T, Ho A, Neugebauer R, Pratt I, Warfield A (2003) Xen and the art of virtualization. In: Proceedings of symposium on operating systems principles

Becher M, Dornseif M, Klein CN (2005) FireWire all your memory are belong to us. In: Proceedings of CanSecWest

Bil (2009) Service billing is hard. http://perspectives.mvdirona.com/2009/02/16/ServiceBillingIsHard.aspx

Checkoway S, Shacham HIa (2013) Why the system call API is a bad untrusted RPC interface. In: Proceedings of international conference on architectural support for programming languages and operating systems

Chen C, Maniatis P, Perrig A, Vasudevan A, Sekar V (2013) Towards verifiable resource accounting for outsourced computation. In: Proceedings of the 9th ACM SIGPLAN/SIGOPS international conference on virtual execution environments. ACM, New York, pp 167–178. http://doi.acm.org/10.1145/2451512.2451546

Cohen R (2019) Navigating the fog-billing, metering and measuring the cloud. Cloud Comput J http://cloudcomputing.sys-con.com/node/858723

Falliere N, Murchu LO, Chien E (2011) W32.stuxnet dossier, version 1:3. Symantec, Cupertino

Gong L (2018) Java 2 platform security architecture. http://docs.oracle.com/javase/6/docs/technotes/guides/security/spec/security-spec.doc.html

IDC (2013) IT cloud services user survey: top benefits and challenges. http://blogs.idc.com/ie/?p=210

Intel Corporation (2008) Intel trusted execution technology: software development guide. Document number 315168-005

Iyer R, Illikkal R, Zhao L, Newell D, Moses J (2009) Virtual platform architectures for resource metering in datacenters. ACM, New York, pp 89–90

Kurts T, Surgutchik R, Lempel O, Anati I, Lustig H (2003) Method and apparatus for branch trace message scheme. US Patent 6,647,545

Lampson B (2009) Usable security: how to get it. Commun ACM 52(11):25–27

Li Y, McCune J, Newsome J, Perrig A, Baker B, Drewry W (2014) MiniBox: a two-way sandbox for x86 native code. In: 2014 USENIX annual technical conference (USENIX ATC 14). USENIX Association, Philadelphia, pp 409–420. https://www.usenix.org/conference/atc14/technical-sessions/presentation/li_yanlin

Liu M, Ding X (2010) On trustworthiness of CPU usage metering and accounting. IEEE Computer Society, Washington, pp 82–91. https://doi.org/10.1109/ICDCSW.2010.40

Matrosov A, Rodionov E, Harley D, Malch J (2019) Stuxnet under the microscope. http://www.eset.com/us/resources/white-papers/Stuxnet_Under_the_Microscope.pdf

McCune JM, Perrig A, Seshadri A, van Doorn L (2007) Turtles all the way down: research challenges in user-based attestation. In: USENIX workshop on hot topics in security

McCune JM, Li Y, Qu N, Zhou Z, Datta A, Gligor VD, Perrig A (2010) TrustVisor: efficient TCB reduction and attestation. In: 31st IEEE symposium on security and privacy, S&P 2010, 16–19 May 2010, Berkeley/Oakland, California, USA, pp 143–158. https://doi.org/10.1109/SP.2010.17

Meserve J (2007) Staged cyber attack reveals vulnerability in power grid. http://edition.cnn.com/2007/US/09/26/power.at.risk/index.html

Mihoob A, Molina-Jimenez C, Shrivastava S (2010) A case for consumer-centric resource accounting models. In: Proceedings international conference on cloud computing

Mogul JC (2005) Operating systems should support business change. USENIX Association, Berkeley, pp 8–8. http://portal.acm.org/citation.cfm?id=1251123.1251131

Peinado M, Chen Y, England P, Manferdelli J (2004) NGSCB: a trusted open system. In: 9th Australian conference on information security and privacy

Seshadri A, Luk M, Qu N, Perrig A (2007) SecVisor: a tiny hypervisor to provide lifetime kernel code integrity for commodity OSes. In: Proceedings of the 21st ACM symposium on operating systems principles 2007, SOSP 2007, Stevenson, Washington, USA, October 14–17, 2007, pp 335–350. https://doi.org/10.1145/1294261.1294294

Sha (2011) Cloud storage providers need sharper billing metrics. http://www.networkworld.com/news/2011/061711-cloud-storage-providers-need-sharper.html?page=2

Shachtman N (2011) Exclusive: computer virus hits U.S. drone fleet. http://www.wired.com/dangerroom/2011/10/virus-hits-drone-fleet/

Somorovsky J, Heiderich M, Jensen M, Schwenk J, Gruschka N, Lo Iacono L (2011) All your clouds are belong to us—security analysis of cloud management interfaces. ACM, New York, pp 3–14. http://doi.acm.org/10.1145/2046660.2046664

Vasco (2011) DigiNotar reports security incident. http://www.vasco.com/company/about_vasco/press_room/news_archive/2011/news_diginotar_reports_security_incident.aspx

Vasudevan A, Qu N, Perrig A (2011) XTRec: secure real-time execution trace recording on commodity platforms. In: Proceedings of the 44th Hawaii international conference on systems science (HICSS-44 2011), 4–7 January 2011, Koloa, Kauai, HI, USA, pp 1–10. https://doi.org/10.1109/HICSS.2011.500

Vasudevan A, Parno B, Qu N, Gligor VD, Perrig A (2012) Lockdown: towards a safe and practical architecture for security applications on commodity platforms. In: Proceedings of the trust and trustworthy computing-5th international conference, TRUST 2012, Vienna, Austria, 13–15 June 2012, pp 34–54. https://doi.org/10.1007/978-3-642-30921-2_3

Wachs M, Xu L, Kanevsky A, Ganger GR (2011) Exertion-based billing for cloud storage access. USENIX Association, Berkeley, pp 7–11. http://dl.acm.org/citation.cfm?id=2170444.2170451

Willems C, Hund R, Fobian A, Felsch D, Holz T, Vasudevan A (2012) Down to the bare metal: using processor features for binary analysis. In: 28th Annual computer security applications conference, ACSAC 2012, Orlando, 3–7 December 2012, pp 189–198. https://doi.org/10.1145/2420950.2420980

Yee B, Sehr D, Dardyk G, Chen JB, Muth R, Ormandy T, Okasaka S, Narula N, Fullagar N (2009) Native client: a sandbox for portable untrusted x86 native code. In: Proceedings of IEEE symposium on security and privacy

Zhou F, Goel M, Desnoyers P, Sundaram R (2011) Scheduler vulnerabilities and coordinated attacks in cloud computing, pp 123–130. https://doi.org/10.1109/NCA.2011.24

Zhou Z, Gligor VD, Newsome J, McCune JM (2012) Building verifiable trusted path on
    commodity x86 computers. In: 2012 IEEE symposium on security and privacy, pp 616–630.
    https://doi.org/10.1109/SP.2012.42
Zhou Z, Han J, Lin YH, Perrig A, Gligor V (2013) Kiss: key it simple and secure corporate key
    management. https://doi.org/10.1007978-3-642-38908-5-1
Zhou Z, Yu M, Gligor VD (2015) Dancing with giants: Wimpy kernels for on-demand I/O isolation.
    IEEE Secur Priv 13(2):38–46. https://doi.org/10.1109/MSP.2015.26

Printed in the United States
By Bookmasters